CHURCH BELLS

LECTOR HOUSE PUBLIC DOMAIN WORKS

CHURCH BELLS

HENRY BEAUCHAMP WALTERS, PERCY DEARMER

ISBN: 978-93-5420-992-5

Published: 1908

LECTOR HOUSE LLP
E-MAIL: lectorpublishing@gmail.com

Frontispiece.

King David playing on hand-bells.

From a manuscript Psalter in the British Museum. This subject was often
selected for the heading to the forty-sixth Psalm, as here.

(See page 5.)

THE ARTS OF THE CHURCH

CHURCH BELLS

BY

H. B. WALTERS, M.A., F.S.A.

Author of Greek Art, &c.

EDITED BY
THE REV. PERCY DEARMER, M.A.

WITH THIRTY-NINE ILLUSTRATIONS

1908

EDITOR'S NOTE

The little volumes in the ARTS OF THE CHURCH series are intended to provide information in an interesting as well as an accurate form about the various arts which have clustered round the public worship of GOD in the Church of CHRIST. Though few have the opportunity of knowing much about them, there are many who would like to possess the main outlines about those arts whose productions are so familiar to the Christian, and so dear. The authors will write for the average intelligent man who has not had the time to study all these matters for himself; and they will therefore avoid technicalities, while endeavouring at the same time to present the facts with a fidelity which will not, it is hoped, be unacceptable to the specialist.

AUTHOR'S NOTE

Acknowledgements must be expressed to the following persons who have assisted in supplying photographs or other materials for the illustrations to this book: to the Rev. W. H. Frere, Mr. A. Riley, and the Committee of the Alcuin Club for permission to reproduce in plate 4 a page of a MS. Pontifical; to Dr. Amherst D. Tyssen and the Rev. Dr. Jessopp for blocks; to W. Watson, Esq., of York, and Miss Wilson of Idbury for photographs; to Messrs. Wills and Hepworth of Loughborough, Messrs. Mears and Stainbank, and Messrs. Taylor and Co. of Loughborough for blocks, negatives and photographs.

CONTENTS

Chapter   *Page*

Editor's Note vi

Author's Note vii

I. Early History and Methods of Casting. 1

II. The English Bell-founders 10

III. Big Bells; Carillons and Chimes; Campaniles. 20

IV. Change-Ringing 31

V. Uses and Customs of Bells 37

VI. The Decoration of Bells and their Inscriptions 49

VII. The Care of Bells 66

Index 74

LIST OF ILLUSTRATIONS

		Page
I.	King David playing on hand-bells.	iv
II.	Saxon Tower, Earl's Barton, Northants.	2
III.	A performer on hand-bells.	3
IV.	Tower or Turret with Bells	4
V.	The blessing of two bells newly hung in a church tower.	7
VI.	Late Norman bell-turret (about 1180) at Wyre Church, Worcestershire.	9
VII.	Inner moulds or cores for casting a ring of eight bells.	11
VIII.	Outer moulds or copes for casting a ring of eight bells.	12
IX.	Moulds ready for casting.	14
X.	Forming the Mould.	16
XI.	Running the Molten Metal.	18
XII.	The Mortar of Friar Towthorpe.	19
XIII.	Bell by an early fourteenth-century London founder.	21
XIV.	Blessing the Donor of the Bell.	23
XV.	Stamps used by London Founders.	24
XVI.	Bell by Robert Mot of London (1575–1600),	27
XVII.	A ring of eight bells.	28
XVIII.	The 9th bell of Loughborough Parish Church.	30
XIX.	The tenor bell of Exeter Cathedral, called "Grandison."	33
XX.	"Great John of Beverley."	35

XXI.   The great bell of Tong Church, Shropshire. 38

XXII.   "Great Paul." 40

XXIII.   The old "Great Tom" of Westminster. 42

XXIV.   The Belfry of Bruges. 43

XXV.   The Campanile or Bell-Tower of Chichester Cathedral. 45

XXVI.   The old Campanile of King's College, Cambridge. 47

XXVII.   The "Bell House" in the Churchyard at East Bergholt, Suffolk. . . .50

XXVIII.   Diagram showing method of hanging a bell for ringing 51

XXIX.   Peal of Eight Bells (Tenor 16 cwt.) for Aberavon Church, Glamorganshire. 52

XXX.   Ringers at S. Paul's Cathedral Ringing a Peal on New Year's Eve on the Twelve Bells. 55

XXXI.   The Ringing of the Sacring Bell by a Clerk in Minor Orders. 57

XXXII.   Sacring Bell hung on Rood-Screen, Scarning Church, Norfolk. . . .59

XXXIII.   Ancient Sanctus Bell (Fourteenth Century). 61

XXXIV.   Tower of Waltham Abbey Church, Essex. 62

XXXV.   Symbols of the Four Evangelists. 65

XXXVI.   Bell by John Tonne, a Founder of Henry VIII's time (1520–1540). Ornamented in the French fashion. 67

XXXVII.   Specimens of Gothic capital letters. 68

XXXVIII.   Specimens of "Mixed Gothic" lettering. 70

XXXIX.   Part of a Seventeenth Century Bell by Henry Oldfield of Nottingham. 72

CHURCH BELLS

CHAPTER I

EARLY HISTORY AND METHODS OF CASTING.

The origin of the bell as an instrument of music is, one may almost say, lost in antiquity. Its use is, moreover, widely spread over the whole world. But I do not propose to enlarge on its early history here, or on its employment by all nations, Christian or heathen. Space will not permit me to do more than trace its history and uses in the Christian Church, and more particularly in the Church of England.

The word "bell" is said to be connected with "bellow" and "bleat" and to refer to its sound; the later Latin writers call it, among other names, *campana*, a word with which we are familiar, not only as frequently occurring in old bell inscriptions, but as forming part of the word "Campanalogy," or the science of bell-ringing. The French and Germans, again, call it *cloche* and *glocke* respectively, the words being the same as our "clock"; but that is a later use, and they really mean "cloak," with reference to the shape of the bell, or rather of the mould in which it is cast. Modern bell-founders, it is interesting to note, speak of the mould as the *cope*, which again suggests a connection with the form of a garment.

It is not known exactly when bells were introduced into the Christian Church; but it is certain that large bells of the form with which we are familiar were not invented until after some centuries of Christianity. The small and often clandestine congregations of the ages of persecution needed no audible signal to call them together; but with the advent of peaceful times, and the growth of the congregations, some method of summons doubtless came to be considered necessary. Their invention is sometimes ascribed to Paulinus, Bishop of Nola, in Italy, about A.D. 400; sometimes to Pope Sabinianus (A.D. 604), the successor of Gregory the Great. At all events, from the beginning of the seventh century notices of bells of some size become frequent. The Venerable Bede in 680 brought a bell from Italy to place in his Abbey at Wearmouth, and mentions one as being then used at Whitby Abbey. About 750, we read that Egbert, Archbishop of York, ordered the priests to toll bells at the appointed hours. Ingulphus, the chronicler of Croyland Abbey, mentions that a peal of seven bells was put up there in the tenth century, and that there was not such a harmonious peal in the whole of England; which implies that rings of bells were then common. If any doubt on the matter still remained, it would be dispelled by the existence to this day of some hundred church towers dating from the Saxon period, and evidently, by their size and construction, intended to hold rings of bells (Plate 1).

Plate 1.

Photo by] *[C. Law.*

Saxon Tower, Earl's Barton, Northants.
A tower built in the first half of the eleventh century
and intended to contain bells.

(See page 2.)

I speak of "rings of bells"—and that is a more correct term than "peal," which refers to the sound they make—but it must be remembered that in those days bells were not rung as in modern times. At best they were "chimed," i.e., sounded without being rung up; but change-ringing, which implies the full swinging round of the bell through a complete circle, so that the clapper strikes twice in each revolution, was only introduced in the seventeenth century, and moreover has always been peculiar to this country.

Plate 2.

A performer on hand-bells.

From a MS. Missal in the British Museum.

(See page 2.)

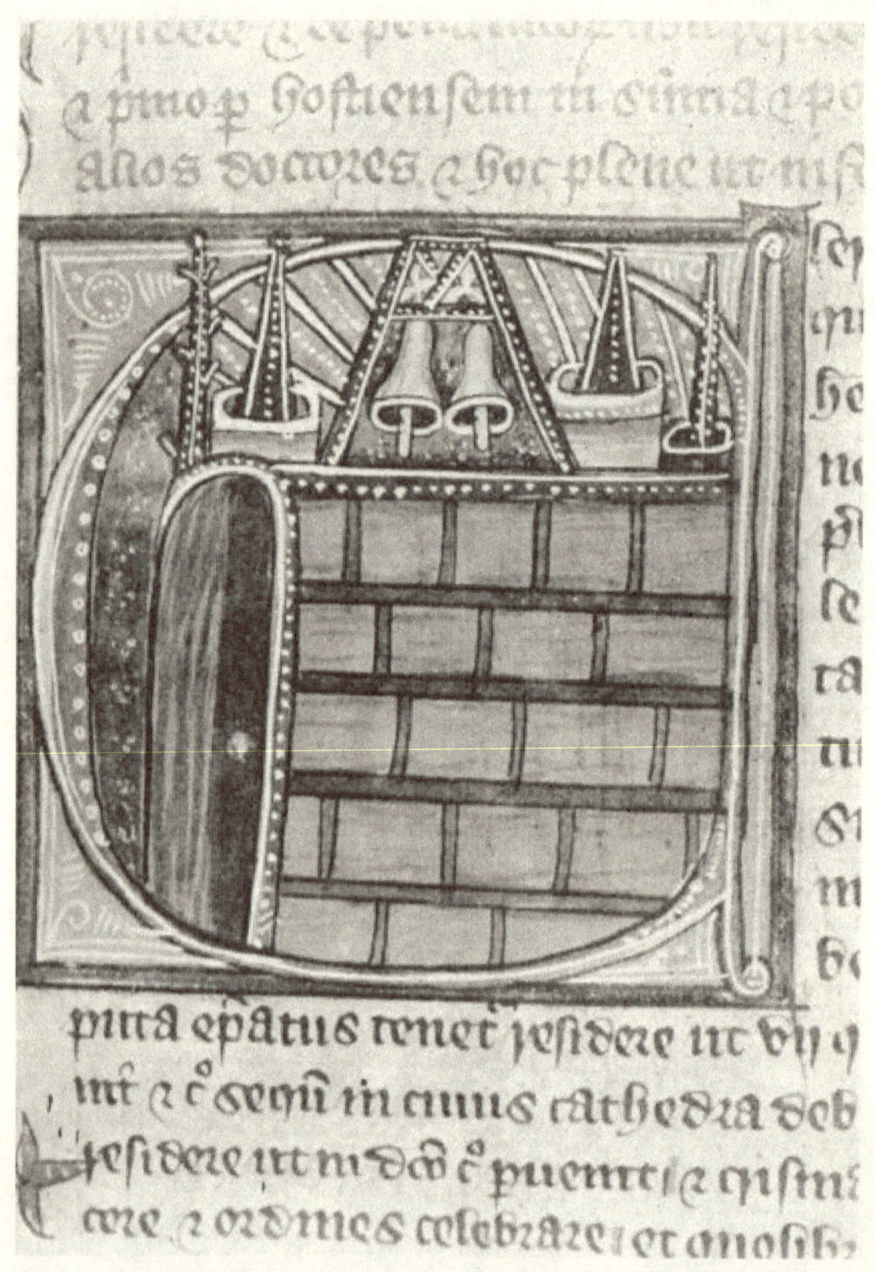

Tower or Turret with Bells

From a manuscript in the British Museum.

Two bells hung in a church tower or turret; the method of hanging not shown.

(See page 5.)

Several ancient manuscripts have pictures which throw light on the use of bells in early times, as, for instance, one which depicts a performer on a row of small "hand-bells" suspended from an arch, which he strikes with a hammer (Plate 2). Another portrays King David engaged in a similar act (Frontispiece); and others give representations of church towers or turrets with bells hanging in them, apparently without wheels or ringing arrangements (Plate 3). In the Bayeux tapestry there is a representation of the funeral of Edward the Confessor, in which the corpse is accompanied by two boys, each ringing a pair of hand-bells.

Ancient bells were invariably dedicated with elaborate ceremonies, and were baptized with the name of the saint or other person after whom they were named (Plate 4). The bells at Croyland, just mentioned, were named Pega, Bega, Turketyl, Tatwin, Bartholomew, Betelin, and Guthlac. There is, however, much disputing as to the exact ceremonies employed, some authorities maintaining that bells were neither baptized nor even "washed," but merely blessed and consecrated, so as to be set apart from all secular uses.

In the Norman and early Plantagenet period the use of bells must have been generally recognized. In London we hear of one Alwoldus, a *campanarius* (1150), which can only mean "bell-founder." And as early as the reign of Richard I the Guild of Saddlers were granted the privilege of ringing the bells of the Priory of S. Martin-le-Grand on the occasion of their bi-weekly masses in the church. The priory was also entitled to claim the sum of 8*d.* for ringing at the funeral of deceased members of the Guild. Some of the bell-cotes of our smaller parish churches, as at Northborough in Northants and Manton, Rutland, appear to date from the Norman period (Plate 5). In the twelfth century Prior Conrad gave five large bells to Canterbury Cathedral, and in 1050 there were seven at Exeter; to ring the former no less than sixty-three men were required!

But these are all mere historical records, and it may be of more interest to know whether any bells of this remote date still exist in England. With one or two exceptions, bells did not begin to bear inscriptions until the fourteenth century, and even then we do not find dates upon them. The only early-dated bells in England are at Claughton, in Lancashire (1296), and Cold Ashby, Northants (1317). There are, however, here and there bells of a peculiar shape which it is possible to assign to a period previous to the fourteenth century. They are long and cylindrical in form, with hemispherical or square heads, and usually very unpleasing in tone, as the straight sides check vibration. One such bell, formerly in Worcester Cathedral, and now in the possession of Lord Amherst of Hackney, must belong to the ring put up by Bishop Blois in 1220 in honour of our LORD and His Mother. Even more remarkable is a bell at Caversfield in Oxfordshire, dedicated "in honour of S. Lawrence," a long inscription on the edge showing that it was given by Hugh Gargate, Lord of the Manor in the reign of King John (about 1210), and Sybilla his wife. Such an inscription is very rare at this early date; and it is interesting to note that it is in plain Roman or Saxon capital letters, whereas all the later inscribed bells have what are known as Gothic or Lombardic letters, which came in about the end of the thirteenth century. Most counties possess examples of these long, narrow bells; they are specially common in Shropshire and Northumberland.

The earliest bells were probably not cast, but made of metal plates riveted together, like the modern cow-bell. Not a few bells of this kind have been unearthed at different times, but they are all mere hand-bells of very remote date, i.e., before the Norman Conquest, and the process of casting must have been introduced in very early times into England.

Bell-metal is a compound of copper and tin, in varying proportions, but usually three to four parts of copper to one part of tin. The former metal adds strength and tenacity to the bell, the latter brings out its tone. The popular superstition that silver improves the tone of bells is not only entirely baseless, but in point of fact it has just the opposite effect! The numerous stories which are current, of silver being thrown into bells at their casting, of which Great Tom of Lincoln is an example, must therefore be discredited. In recent years steel bells have been made by one English firm, but they are only one degree less objectionable than the tubes of metal which are sometimes also dignified by the name.

The process of casting a bell, as employed both by ancient and modern founders, may be described somewhat as follows: — The first business is the construction of the core, a hollow cone of brick somewhat smaller than the inner diameter of the intended bell, over which is plastered a specially-prepared mixture of clay, bringing it up to the exact size and shape of the interior of the bell. This was usually modelled with the aid of a wooden "crook," something like a pair of compasses; but is now done with an iron framework called a "sweep," which revolves on a pivot and moulds the core by means of metal blades. This clay mould is then baked hard by means of a fire lighted within it. The next stage was the construction of the cope or outer casing of the mould, which used to be also made in hard clay, its inner surface following the *outer* shape and dimensions of the bell. The "thickness" of the bell itself, i.e., the part to be occupied by the molten metal, was formed in a friable composition which was laid over the core and then destroyed. In modern times the "thickness" has been dispensed with, the cope being formed by lining a casing of cast iron with clay shaped to the external form and dimensions of the bell. The mould is now complete, except for providing for the cannons or metal loops which attach the bell to the stock, and the loop to which the clapper is suspended inside. Every care having been taken to adjust the respective positions of the cope and core with exactness, the molten metal is then poured in through an opening, and left to cool, after which the bell comes out complete. The process is analogous to that known as *cire perdu*, employed by sculptors for the casting of bronze statues. Illustrations of the moulding processes are given in Plates 6–10.

Inscriptions and ornaments are produced in relief on the bell from stamps, also in relief, which are pressed into the mould, making a hollow impression in it. Copies of coins were often produced in this way by the older founders. Down to about the end of the seventeenth century each letter, or sometimes each word, was placed on a separate *patera* or tablet of metal. The usual place for the inscription is just below the "shoulder"-angle; but modern founders prefer the middle or "waist."

The blessing of two bells newly hung in a church tower.

From a MS. Pontifical of the fifteenth century.

(See page 5.)

A very interesting illustration of these processes is given in the famous bell-founder's window in the north aisle of York Minster, dating from the fourteenth century, part of which is here reproduced. The window is divided into three lights, each having five compartments, and in each light is a large principal subject surrounded by ornamentation in the form of bells, grotesque animals, and other devices, with two rows of bells hanging in trefoil-headed arches above. In the central compartment of the middle light (Plate 13) the subject is the blessing by an archbishop of the bell-founder, who kneels in a supplicating attitude; in his hands is a scroll inscribed with his name, RICHARD TUNNOC, and under the canopy above the group a bell is suspended.

The other two lights have as their main subjects scenes from the actual processes of bell-founding. In the left-hand light (Plate 9) we have the forming of the inner mould or "core," as already described. One figure is turning it with a handle like that of a grindstone, while another moulds the clay to its proper form with a long crooked tool. The core rests on two trestles, between the legs of which two completed bells are seen; above are a bell and a scroll with the founder's name. In the right-hand window (Plate 10) are three figures engaged in running the molten metal, which is coloured red. The metal is kept heated in the furnace by means of bellows, worked by two boys, while the chief workman watches the molten stream running into the mould.

The next process, in the case of a "ring" of bells, is the tuning which is generally necessary, though sometimes the founder is fortunate enough to turn out what is known as a "maiden peal." Formerly this was done by chipping the inside of the bell or cutting away the edge of the lip. But it is now more effectively accomplished by a vertical lathe, driven by steam. The modern bell-founder can attain to much greater exactness in this respect, because it is now recognized that there is a regular ratio between the weight of a bell and its diameter, and that a certain size or weight implies a certain musical note. Thus for a ring of eight in the key of F, the weight of the tenor would be 14 cwt., and its diameter at the mouth reckoned at 42 inches, the treble 5 cwt., and its diameter 29 inches.

The frames are made separately, and the bells hung on them in the tower with their headstocks already attached[1]; until recently all these fittings were made of wood, and iron or brass were only used for the smaller parts, but it is now the custom of some founders to employ iron frames, and even iron stocks, which may be an improvement in lightness and stability, or for ringing purposes, but are hardly so in appearance.

---

[1] For an illustration of bells in a frame, see Plate 28.

Plate 5.

Photo by]   [*J. Glover, Pershore.*

Late Norman bell-turret (about 1180) at Wyre Church, Worcestershire.

There are openings for two bells, but only one is now used.

(See page 5.)

CHAPTER II

THE ENGLISH BELL-FOUNDERS

In early mediaeval times it is probable that bell-founding was largely the work of the monastic orders. It was regarded rather as a fine art than a trade, and ecclesiastics seem to have vied in producing the most ingenious and recondite Latin rhyming verses to adorn their bells. S. Dunstan, whose skill as a smith is familiar to all, is known to have been instrumental in hanging, if not in casting bells; and at Canterbury he gave careful directions for their correct use. S. Ethelwold, Bishop of Winchester 963–984, cast bells for Abingdon Abbey. In the museum at York there is a mortar of bell-metal cast by Friar William de Towthorpe, with the date 1308 (Plate 11); but this belongs to later times, when a class of professional founders had sprung up, and is therefore exceptional. We read, however, of Sir William Corvehill, a monk of Wenlock Priory, who died shortly after its dissolution, in 1546, that he "could make organs, clocks, and chimes," and was "a good bell-founder and maker of the frames for bells." It has not been possible to trace his work in any existing bells.

From time to time, however, we hear of professional bell-founders, as they may be termed, and even in the thirteenth century foundries appear to have been started in London, Bristol, Gloucester, and York. The London "belleyeteres," as they are called, early attained a position of importance. Many of them are mentioned in contemporary records of the fourteenth century; of others we have the existing wills, which enable us to trace the succession from one generation to another; and again the names of several occur on bells of this period, contrary to the usual mediaeval practice. In the days when work for the Church was a labour of love, less importance was attached to self-advertisement; though the student of the past may regret this in some measure if it deprives him of information he wishes to acquire.

The first London founders of note were a family of the name of Wymbish, residing in Aldgate, which was always the bell-founders' quarter, as the still existing name of Billiter (or Belleyetere) Street implies. There were three Wymbishes—Richard, Michael, and Walter—covering the period 1290–1310. Richard cast bells for the neighbouring Priory of the Holy Trinity, and has left his name at Goring, in Oxfordshire, and on other bells in Essex, Kent, Northants, and Suffolk; Michael cast five bells still remaining in Bucks; and Walter, one in Sussex. Other important founders of this century are Peter de Weston, William Revel, and William Burford.[2] John and William Rufford, who may have had their foundry at Bedford,

[2] An early London bell is illustrated on Plate 12.

were known as "Royal bell-founders," and placed upon their bells the heads of the reigning King, Edward III, and his consort, Philippa. These stamps have a very curious history; and were successively the property of founders at King's Lynn, Worcester, Leicester, and Nottingham. At the latter place they remained in use from about 1400 down to the end of the eighteenth century; and their last appearance is in 1806, on a bell at Waltham Abbey, cast by Briant of Hertford.

Plate 6.

Inner moulds or cores for casting a ring of eight bells.

(See page 6.)

Outer moulds or copes for casting a ring of eight bells.

(See page 6.)

Between 1370 and 1385 there was a founder in Kent whose name was Stephen Norton; he used very richly-ornamented letters, which may be seen on one of the old bells of Worcester Cathedral, cast by him when the tower was rebuilt. The other principal foundries of this century were at King's Lynn, Gloucester, and York.

The Gloucester foundry was successively in the hands of "Sandre of Gloucester" (1300–1320) and "Master John of Gloucester" (1340–1350). The latter's reputation apparently extended to East Anglia, as in 1347 he was commissioned to cast six new bells for the Cathedral at Ely, which were conveyed thither from Northampton by way of the Nene and Ouse. The largest bell, called "Iᴇsvs," weighed nearly two tons, and the fourth was named "Walsingham," after the famous Prior Alan who constructed the central octagon of the cathedral.

Of the York founders, the most famous is Richard Tunnoc, commemorated in the remarkable "Bell-founder's window" already described (Plate 13). He was M.P. for the city in 1327, and died in 1330. The names of other known founders of this city extend from Johannes de Copgrave, in 1150, down to the time of the Reformation. A bell at Scawton, in the North Riding, has been thought to be the work of Copgrave, and, if so, is by far the earliest existing church bell in England, if not in Europe.

In the fifteenth century (with which we may include the whole period down to the Reformation) the bell-foundries increase not only in importance but in numbers; and those already mentioned find rivals springing up at Reading and Wokingham, Exeter, Bristol, Leicester, Norwich, Nottingham, Bury St. Edmunds, Salisbury, and Worcester. The character of the inscriptions now changes, and in most cases (though not invariably) we find "black-letter smalls," with initial capitals, substituted for the old Gothic capitals used throughout. There is also a great increase in the number and variety of the crosses and other ornamental devices used by the founders, and many introduce foundry-shields or trade-marks, with quasi-heraldic or punning devices.

The London foundries, however, still maintain their place at the head of the craft, and their bells are found all over England from Northumberland to Cornwall. Two founders of the fifteenth century, Henry Jordan and John Danyell, whose date is about 1450–1470, cast between them about two hundred bells still existing. These are adorned with some beautiful and ingenious devices, such as an elegant cross surrounded by the words *iḥu merci laḍi ḥelp* (Plate 14) and the Royal Arms surmounted by a crown. Jordan's foundry-shield bears, among other devices, a bell and a laver-pot as symbolical of his trade, and a dolphin with reference to his membership of the Fishmongers' Company. Another remarkable device (Plate 14) is that used by William Culverden (1510–1523), with a rebus on his name (*culver* = "pigeon"). Thomas Bullisdon is remarkable as having cast a ring of five bells for the Priory of S. Bartholomew in Smithfield about 1510, all of which still exist there.

To tell of the works of Roger Landen of Wokingham, Robert Hendley of Gloucester, John of Stafford (a Leicester founder), Robert Norton of Exeter, or the Brasyers of Norwich, would require a volume. I can only note some interesting features of their work. The Brasyers seem to have been the most successful workers outside London, and no less than one hundred and fifty of their bells still exist in Norfolk. Their trade-mark was a shield with three bells and a crown, which after the Reformation went to the Leicester foundry, and some of their inscriptions, in rhyming hexameters, are very beautiful. A Bristol founder of about 1450 used for his mark a ship, the badge of his native city. The Bury founders were also gun-makers, and place on their trade-mark a bell and a cannon, with the crown and crossed arrows of S. Edmund.

Plate 8.

Moulds ready for casting.
The inner and outer moulds clamped together; the molten metal is poured in through an aperture at the top.

(See page 6.)

Very few bells of this period are dated; but we find examples at Worcester, perhaps cast by the monks there, with the dates 1480 and 1482; and at Thirsk (1410), on a bell which is said to have come from Fountains Abbey. There are also some bells in Lincolnshire, dated 1423 and 1431, by an unknown founder, but remarkable for the extraordinary beauty of the lettering (Plate 36). Dated mediaeval bells are more commonly from foreign sources, as at Baschurch, in Shropshire, where is a Dutch bell by Jan van Venlo, dated 1447, which is said to have come from Valle Crucis Abbey. At Whalley Abbey, in Lancashire, is a Belgian bell of 1537, by Peter van den Ghein, and at Duncton, in Sussex, a French bell dated 1369.

The period of the Reformation, down to about 1600, was, as has been said, "a real bad time for bell-founders," and several of the important foundries, as at Bristol, Gloucester, and elsewhere, appear either to have been closed for a time or died out altogether. The chief cause of this was doubtless the dissolution of the monasteries, coupled with the operations of Edward VI's commissioners, large numbers of bells being sold or converted into secular property. These were distributed among the parish churches, and many instances may be traced of second-hand bells still existing, as at Abberley, in Worcestershire, where there is an ancient bell from a Yorkshire monastery. It should also be remembered that very little church-building was done in the latter half of the century. On the other hand, the statement which has gained some currency, that the commissioners only left one bell in each parish church, is not borne out by facts. Many churches still possess three or even four mediaeval bells which must have hung untouched in their towers before and since the reign of Edward VI.

But this lapse in bell-founding was not invariable; the foundries at Leicester, Nottingham, Bury St. Edmunds, and Reading actually seem to have received a new lease of life, and 1560–1600 is almost their most flourishing period. This is especially the case at Leicester, where a well-known family named Newcombe were at work, succeeded by an equally celebrated founder named Hugh Watts, whose fine bells were deservedly famous. At Nottingham we have the dynasty of the Oldfields, lasting from 1550 to 1710; and at Reading a series of founders of different names, ending in a succession of Knights down to 1700. The Hatches of Ulcombe, in Kent, were another prosperous family, as were the Eldridges of Chertsey.

At Bury St. Edmunds, one Stephen Tonne reigned from 1560 to 1580. His foundry was, however, destined to yield to the sway of that at Colchester, which begins with Richard Bowler about 1590, and reached its culmination between 1620 and 1640, under the great Miles Graye, who has been called "the prince of bell-founders." Numbers of his bells remain in Essex and Suffolk, his masterpiece being, by common consent of ringers, the tenor at Lavenham, in Suffolk. At Colchester, as in other foundries, the seven years of storm and stress—1642–1649—while the Civil War between Charles I and the Parliament raged in England, practically put an end to bell-founding. Siege and other troubles certainly hastened the end of old Miles Graye, who died in 1649, worn out by privation and bodily suffering. His grandson Miles kept on the foundry until 1686.

Forming the Mould.

Part of the Bell Founder's Window in York Minster.

(See page 8.)

Turning to the West of England, we find the foundries at Bristol, Gloucester, Worcester, and Salisbury still in a flourishing condition. At Bristol George Purdue, a native of Taunton, was followed by Roger and William Purdue in the seventeenth century; the latter migrated to Salisbury about 1655, where he carried on the work of John Wallis and John Danton. Thomas Purdue, the last of the family, died at Closworth, in Somerset, in 1711, and on his tombstone are the words—

> "HERE LIES A BELLFOUNDER, HONEST AND TRUE,
> UNTIL THE RESURRECTION, NAMED PURDUE."

In the West of England their place was filled by the Penningtons of Exeter, the Evanses of Chepstow, and the Bilbies of Chew-Stoke, Somerset. The Keenes of Bedford and Woodstock, John Palmer of Gloucester, and John Martin of Worcester, all did good work in their day, as did the Cliburys of Wellington, in Shropshire. Another important Midland firm was that of the Bagleys, of Chacomb, in Northamptonshire, whose foundry was opened in 1631, and flourished till the end of the eighteenth century; though in the latter period its owners became restless, and settled temporarily in London, Witney, and other places. In the North, York was again the chief bell-founding centre, and Samuel Smith and the Sellers were famous exponents of the art; in the East of England we have, besides Miles Graye, first the Brends of Norwich, then John Darbie of Ipswich, and Thomas Gardiner of Sudbury.

Several founders between 1560 and 1700 were mere journeymen, who went about from place to place, doing jobs where they could. Of such was Michael Darbie, of whom it is said, "one specimen of his casting seems to have been enough for a neighbourhood." At Blewbury, in Berkshire, a local man attempted to recast a bell in 1825. He failed twice, but was then successful, and placed on his work the appropriate motto, *Nil desperandum*. Apart from this, it was not at all uncommon for bells to be cast on the spot, as were Great Tom of Lincoln and the great bell of Canterbury, or at some convenient intermediate place.

In 1684 a fresh start was given to the Gloucester foundry, then fallen on bad days, by Abraham Rudhall, perhaps the most successful founder England has known. He and his descendants cast altogether 4,521 bells down to 1830, and their fame spread all over the West of England, from Cornwall to Lancashire, and even over the seas. Most of the big rings of bells in the West Midlands are their work. The foundry finally came to an end in 1835, when the business was bought up by Mears of London.

In London itself bell-founding seems to have come almost to an end between 1530 and 1570. But about the latter year arose one Robert Mot, who set on foot what is now the oldest-established business of any kind in England. The foundry in the Whitechapel Road, now only a short distance removed from its original home, has always upheld its reputation throughout the three hundred years and more during which it has been continuously worked. Several of Mot's bells still remain in London, and many others in Kent and Essex (Plate 15). In the seventeenth century the foundry was in the hands of Anthony and James Bartlet, who cast many bells for Wren's churches after the Great Fire. In the eighteenth, under Phelps, Lester, Pack, and Chapman, successively, its reputation gradually increased, and in 1783 began a dynasty of Mearses lasting down to 1870. The name is still preserved by the firm of Mears and Stainbank, though neither a Mears nor a Stainbank now owns a share in the business. An illustration of their bells is given in Plate 16.

Plate 10.

Running the Molten Metal.

Part of the Bell Founder's Window in York Minster.

(See page 8.)

Their great rivals of modern times, the Taylors of Loughborough, cannot emulate them in antiquity, though they can still boast a respectable pedigree, dating from Thomas Eayre of Kettering, in 1731. After moving to S. Neots, Leicester, and Oxford, the firm finally settled, about 1840, under John Taylor, at Loughborough, where his grandsons now carry on the business. Illustrations of their bells are given in Plates 17–21.

Plate 11.

The Mortar of Friar Towthorpe.

(See page 10.)

CHAPTER III

BIG BELLS; CARILLONS AND CHIMES; CAMPANILES

Bells of exceptional size, styled in Latin *Signa*, are no new invention of the founder's art. It speaks much for the skill of the mediaeval craftsman that he should have been able to cast giant bells which not only rivalled the *chefs-d'oeuvre* of our own day, but, as objects of beauty, certainly surpassed them.

In the twelfth century a "tenor" was added by Prior Wybert to Prior Conrad's great ring of five at Canterbury Cathedral, which bell, it is said, took thirty-two men to ring it. (This was achieved by placing them on a plank fastened to a stock, by which means it was set in motion.) It was, however, surpassed by another cast in 1316, in memory of S. Thomas of Canterbury. This weighed over 3½ tons, but was broken in the fall of the campanile, 1382, and was replaced in 1459 by a slightly heavier bell, cast in London, and dedicated in honour of S. Dunstan. Its successor, a re-casting by Lester and Pack of London, in 1762, stills hangs in the south-west tower, and is used for the clock and for tolling.

The cathedral of Exeter was furnished with two bells which deserve the title of great; but one, the tenor of the old ring of seven, does not strictly come within the limits of this chapter, which deals with single bells. All these old bells had names, some derived from their donors, and the tenor was called Grandison, from the bishop by whom it was given about 1360. Its successor, cast in 1902, by Taylor of Loughborough, weighs about 3 tons (Plate 18). The other, Great Peter of Exeter, hangs in the north tower, and was the gift of Bishop Peter (Courtenay) in 1484. It has been twice re-cast, and the present bell is the work of the Thomas Purdue mentioned in the previous chapter, dated 1676. The founder attempted to preserve the old mediaeval inscription,

𝔓lebs patriæ plaudit dum petrum plenius audit
"The people of the country applaud when they hear Peter's full sound,"

but only found room for the first five words. From the style of the inscription we gather that it was originally cast at the Exeter foundry. Its weight is given as 6¼ tons, but according to another estimate is not more than four.

There is a rival "Great Peter" at Gloucester, and here the original bell still survives, the only mediaeval *signum* which we still possess. It bears the inscription,

𝔐e fecit fieri conventus nomine petri
"The monastery had me made in Peter's name,"

together with two shields, one charged with three bells, the other with the arms of the abbey. It may have been cast by the monks, as it bears no known foundry-stamps, but the expression "had me made" seems to imply otherwise. Its weight is 2 tons 18 cwt. Yet another, but a modern "Great Peter," is that of York Minster, cast in 1845, and weighing 12½ tons. It is the second largest church bell in England.

Plate 12.

Bell by an early fourteenth-century London founder.
With inscription in Gothic capitals.

(See page 10.)

From "Great Peters" we pass to "Great Toms." Of these there are two famous examples, one at Lincoln Cathedral, the other at Christ Church, Oxford. The Lincoln Tom, which hangs in the central tower of the cathedral, does not appear in records before 1610, in which year it was re-cast by Henry Oldfield of Nottingham, and Robert Newcombe of Leicester. It was cast in the minster yard, and weighed 4 tons 8 cwt. In course of time it was found to be too heavy for the tower, and was "clocked," or tied down, as a contemporary journalist describes it, in 1802: "He has been chained and riveted down, so that instead of the full mouthful he hath been used to send forth, he is enjoined in the future merely to wag his tongue." The result was inevitable, and in 1827 "he" was reported cracked, which led to his being re-cast by Mears of Whitechapel in 1835.

Great Tom of Christ Church, which now hangs in the tower over the gateway, originally came to the newly-founded "HOUSE OF CHRIST" from the despoiled Abbey of Oseney. Six other bells were brought with it, of which two still hang in the "meat-safe" belfry. Antony à Wood, the Oxford chronicler, tells us that it bore the inscription:

IN THOMAE LAVDE RESONO BIMBOM SINE FRAVDE
"In the praise of Thomas I sound 'Bimbom' without guile."

Thrice unsuccessfully recast between 1612 and 1680, it is in its present form the work of Christopher Hodson, a London founder, who placed upon it a long inscription beginning with the words, MAGNUS THOMAS (*"Great Tom"*). Oxonians will remember the ringing of the bell every night at nine o'clock.

Among other great bells of historical interest we may mention that which hangs in the south tower of Beverley Minster. It survived from mediaeval times until so recent a date as 1902, when it was re-cast by Messrs. Taylor of Loughborough the weight being no less than 7 tons (Plate 19). The old bell was probably cast at Leicester about 1350, and bore some of the most beautiful lettering ever designed by mediaeval craftsmen (Plate 36). Another of Messrs. Taylor's great works is the great bell of Tong, in Shropshire (Plate 20), originally given by Sir Harry Vernon, in 1518, to be tolled "when any Vernon came to Tong." It was recast in 1720, and again in 1892, its present weight being 2½ tons. It was dedicated to SS. Mary and Bartholomew.

Another great mediaeval bell, only recently recast, deserves mention here, though strictly speaking, the tenor of a ring, and not a *signum*. This is the magnificent tenor at Brailes, in Warwickshire, richly ornamented with shields, crowns, and other devices, cast by John Bird of London, about 1420. It bore a beautiful inscription taken from an old Ascension Day hymn. Greatly to the credit of the local authorities, the inscription and ornaments were exactly reproduced from the old cracked bell on its successor, an admirable piece of work executed in 1877 by Messrs. Blews of Birmingham. The bell weighs about 2 tons.

Blessing the Donor of the Bell.

Part of the Bell Founder's Window in York Minster.

(See page 13.)

Plate 14.

Stamps used by London Founders.

Ornamental Cross used by Henry Jordan of London (1460).

With the words "ihu merci ladi help" and trade mark of William Culverden of London (1510–20), with the words "In d'no co'fido" and a
rebus on his name.

(See pages 13, 49.)

Among great modern bells the hour-bell at Worcester Cathedral, cast by Taylor in 1868, and weighing 4½ tons, deserves special mention, as does a bell at Woburn, Bedfordshire, the work of Mears and Stainbank of London, in 1867, weighing nearly 3 tons. The former bears an inscription taken from Ephesians v. 14, and the letters used are copied from those on the beautiful Lincolnshire fifteenth-century bells mentioned in the previous chapter (p. 15). But the chief masterpiece of recent founding is Messrs. Taylor's "Great Paul" at S. Paul's Cathedral, which holds the reputation of the largest bell in England (Plate 21). It has, however, a rival in the hour-bell of the same cathedral, which has a more lengthy history. There was once at Westminster a famous bell known as "Great Tom," which hung in a clock-tower opposite Westminster Town Hall, but was removed to S. Paul's at the end of the seventeenth century. This bell was famous for its connection with the story told of a sentinel at Windsor Castle in the reign of William III, who was accused of sleeping at his post. He defended himself by stating that he had heard the Westminster bell strike thirteen at midnight, and this brought about his acquittal. Though the truth of the story has often been doubted, the striking thirteen is, mechanically, quite possible. It is said that this bell was originally given by Edward III in honour of the Confessor. On the way to S. Paul's it was cracked by a fall, and eventually it was recast by Richard Phelps, of Whitechapel, in 1716 (Plate 22). It now hangs in the south-west tower, and is used for striking the hour, and for tolling at the death of various great personages. Its weight is 5 tons 4 cwt.

Great Paul is the masterpiece of Messrs. Taylor, "one of Loughborough's glories," says Dr. Raven. It hangs in the same tower, below Phelps' bell, and weighs 16 tons 14 cwt., the diameter at the mouth being 9½ feet. It was cast in 1881, and simply bears the founders' trade-mark and the words (said to have been selected by Canon Liddon) from 1 Corinthians ix. 16:

VAE MIHI SI NON EVANGELISAVERO
"Woe unto me if I preach not the Gospel."

It is used for a few minutes before Sunday services, and at certain other times.

A description of S. Paul's bells is hardly complete without an allusion to the great ring of twelve cast by Taylor in 1877, and placed in the north-west tower, the tenor weighing over 3 tons. They were given by the City Companies and the late Baroness Burdett-Coutts. In addition there are a "service bell," cast in 1700, and two quarter-bells of 1717 for the clock.

Among other great London bells are the ring of ten at the Imperial Institute, cast by Taylor in 1887, and the tenors of the rings at Southwark Cathedral, S. Mary-le-Bow, S. Michael, Cornhill, S. Giles, Cripplegate, and other famous towers; those mentioned are all from rings of twelve, and weigh 2 tons or more.

The old campanile at Westminster, built by Edward III, originally contained three "great bells"; it was pulled down in 1698, and we have followed the history of one of these bells, but the others disappeared. They had no successor until 1856, when the late Lord Grimthorpe (then Mr. Denison), an enthusiast for clocks and bells, designed a great bell for the clock tower of the Houses of Parliament. It was called "Big Ben," either after Sir Benjamin Hall, who was then First Commissioner of Works, or after a noted boxer of the time named Benjamin Brain. Its original founders were Messrs. Warner of London, but being sounded in Palace Yard with a hammer, for the amusement of the public before being hung, it was very soon cracked. In 1857 a new bell was cast by George Mears of Whitechapel, from an improved design, and containing less metal. Its weight is given at 13½ tons. Shortly after its casting Big Ben gave way, but after being quarter-turned, could be once more utilized for striking the hours. Its tone, however, is anything but satisfactory, and one is forced to the opinion that these excessively large bells, very difficult to cast and awkward to manipulate, are apt to prove great mistakes.

CHIMES

Sets of chimes, or arrangements for playing tunes on bells, existed in England even in mediaeval days; but they are nowadays regarded as a speciality of Belgium, and the famous carillons of Antwerp, Bruges, and Mechlin are well known to many a traveller. But it is not our province to speak of these, and it may be of some interest to see what use has been made of such arrangements in England.

Dr. Raven, in his fascinating book, *The Bells of England*, tells us that the machinery of the carillon was a recognized thing in the middle of the fifteenth century, and quotes from the will of John Baret of Bury St. Edmunds, who died in 1463, and gave directions for the playing of a *Requiem aeternum* for his dirge at noon for thirty days after his death, and on each "mind-day," or anniversary, to be continued during the octave. The sexton was also to "take heed to the chimes and wind up the pegs and the plummets" as required. The music of this *Requiem*, we are told, only compassed five notes, and must have been somewhat wearisome to the good people of Bury. In old churchwardens' accounts, as at Ludlow or Warwick, we find frequent references to the repair or upkeep of the chimes.

The principle of the carillon is similar to that of a barrel-organ or musical-box, implying a barrel or drum, set with pegs, and set in motion by being connected with the mechanism of the clock. The pegs, as they turn, raise levers which pull wires in connection with the hammers which strike on the bells. With the ordinary eight bells of an English belfry it is obvious that only a limited choice of tunes within the compass of an octave is possible, and that they can only be played in one key on single notes. The Belgian carillons have sometimes forty or fifty bells in communication with a key-board like that of an organ, and tunes can therefore be played on them in harmony. There are a few carillons of this type in England, the best known being at Boston, in Lincolnshire, and at Cattistock, in Dorset, but usually the ordinary bells are employed, as at Worcester Cathedral and in many towns.

At the Reformation chimes largely died out, but with the Restoration they revived, and we hear of them at Cambridge, Grantham, and elsewhere. Another kind of chime which may here be mentioned is that employed for striking the quarters for the clock. Here, of course, no mechanism is required beyond the connecting-wire which raises the hammer and drops it on the bell. Of such chimes the best known are the Cambridge Quarters, put up in Great S. Mary's Church in 1793. They were composed by Dr. Jowett, the Regius Professor of Laws, assisted by the composer Crotch, who was then only eighteen. The latter is said to have adapted a movement in the opening symphony of Handel's "I know that my Redeemer liveth," for the purpose.

Plate 15.

Bell by Robert Mot of London (1575–1600),

The first owner of the Whitechapel Foundry, where it had been for some years preserved, but is now broken up.

(See page 17.)

Plate 16.

A ring of eight bells.

Recently cast at the Whitechapel Foundry for Uckfield, Sussex.

(See page 18.)

The practice sometimes adopted nowadays of playing hymn tunes on bells by means of ropes tied to the clappers is a miserable substitute for the mechanical contrivance. It not only causes agonies to the musical ear by the unavoidable occurrence of false notes, but is only too likely to lead to the destruction of the bells altogether, as the result of the "clocking," of which I shall have more to say later.

CAMPANILES

We have seen that it is the normal rule in England for bells to be placed in towers forming part of the structure of churches; or rather it should be said that towers for containing the bells were regarded as an essential feature in the construction of a church from the Saxon period onwards. Over the greater part of the Continent the same also holds good; but in Italy we find detached bell-towers, or campaniles, to be of frequent occurrence. The most familiar examples in that country are the campanile of S. Mark's at Venice, and that built by Giotto at Florence. There are many others in Northern Italy, especially at Bologna, and at Ravenna, where the churches are of great antiquity.[3]

Nor are such campaniles altogether unknown in England. In mediaeval times they were attached to several of our cathedral churches, as, for instance, Old S. Paul's, Chichester, Salisbury, and Worcester. The bells of Old S. Paul's were traditionally gambled away by Henry VIII in 1534, and the campanile at Worcester did not survive the Reformation; but that at Salisbury, a most picturesque structure, with a wooden upper storey and spire, was wantonly destroyed in 1777 because the bells were misused! That at Chichester alone remains, a fine Perpendicular erection, at the north-west angle of the cathedral (Plate 24). At King's College, Cambridge, a noble peal of five bells hung in a low wooden belfry on the north side of the chapel, which was destroyed when the bells were sold and melted down in 1754 (Plate 25).

Detached towers are not uncommon features of our parish churches in some parts of England, particularly in Herefordshire and Norfolk. The best examples are at Berkeley, Gloucestershire; Ledbury, Herefordshire; West Walton, Norfolk; and Beccles, Suffolk. Some churches, again, can only boast wooden detached belfries of moderate height to hold their bells, as at Pembridge in Herefordshire, Brooklands in Kent, and East Bergholt in Suffolk (Plate 26). The belfry at the last-named place is no more than a mere shed, and more than one story is told in explanation of the absence of a tower to the otherwise imposing church.

---

[3] The belfry of Bruges is shown in Plate 23.

The 9th bell of Loughborough Parish Church.
Cast by the Taylors of that town.

(See page 19.)

CHAPTER IV

CHANGE-RINGING

One of the chief uses made of church bells in modern times is not strictly a religious use, though it is more or less associated with the Church's seasons, particularly with Sundays and Christmas Day. But it has always been recognized that the secular use of bells, within certain limits, is permissible, as will be further seen in the next chapter.

Change-ringing is, as we have already noted, an entirely modern introduction, and is, moreover, confined to England. In pre-Reformation days we hear of guilds of ringers, as, for instance, at Westminster Abbey, in the reign of Henry III, where the brethren of the guild appear to have enjoyed their privileges since the time of Edward the Confessor. In smaller monastic or collegiate establishments clerics in minor orders were often entrusted with the duty of ringing the bells, as at Tong, in Shropshire (cf. Plate 30). But this kind of ringing was in no way scientific, nor were the fittings of the bells adapted for ringing in the strict modern sense.

The accompanying diagram (Plate 27; compare also Plate 28), showing the way in which a modern bell is hung, will serve to explain the method now adopted for ringing proper, as opposed to chiming. The headstock, or wooden block to which the top of the bell is firmly fixed (so that the bell cannot move independently of it), revolves by means of brass pivots, known as the "gudgeons," in a socket made in the top of the framework. One of these pivots forms the axle of a large wooden wheel, half the circumference of which has a groove for the rope, one end of which is fixed in it, the other passing through a pulley down into the ringing-chamber. In mediaeval times half-wheels only were used, but the complete wheel seems to have been introduced by the fifteenth century, and single bells were "rung" in the sixteenth. Peal-ringing, as we know it, cannot be traced before the seventeenth.

The essential feature of ringing in peal is that the bell shall perform an almost complete revolution each time the rope is pulled, starting from an inverted position. To prevent its falling over again at the conclusion of the stroke, a vertical bar of wood or iron, known as the "stay," is fixed to the side of the stock, which is checked by a movable bar in the lower part of the frame, called the "slider." It is clear that in the course of each revolution the clapper will strike the side twice. Before the invention of the wheel, the bell was merely sounded by means of a lever connecting the rope with the stock, as is still done in ringing small bells, either as "ting-tangs," or when hung in an open turret.

Before the peal can be started, the bells must be rung up or "raised" to the inverted position, which the ringer achieves by a series of steady strokes, each pull increasing in length until it is balanced; at the end of the peal this process is reversed. When bells are merely chimed they are not "raised," but the rope is pulled each time sufficiently to allow one stroke of the clapper. By means of an ingenious apparatus invented by the late Canon Ellacombe, this can now be done by one man if necessary, the muscular effort required being reduced to a minimum.

But change-ringing is a real science, and entails long and assiduous practice and considerable muscular exertion. It is, in fact, one of the best forms of physical exercise conceivable, and must have proved a godsend in that respect to many men whose opportunities would otherwise be limited.

Its elementary principle is, of course, that the bells should be rung in succession, but in a varying order. The method in which the succession varies is the foundation of the various forms known vaguely to most of us as Grandsire Triples, Treble Bob-Major, and so on. They are founded on a recognized arithmetical basis, that of permutations, or the number of arrangements possible of any given number of objects. We know that three letters or numbers can be arranged in six different ways:

$$123 \quad 132$$
$$231 \quad 213$$
$$312 \quad 321$$

Thus, on three bells, only six changes can be rung so as to vary the order each time, and we must then begin over again. With four bells we have a choice of twenty-four changes, which might run as follows:

$$1234 \quad 3124 \quad 4321 \quad 4213$$
$$2134 \quad 1324 \quad 4312 \quad 4231$$
$$2314 \quad 1342 \quad 4132 \quad 2431$$
$$2341 \quad 3142 \quad 1432 \quad 2413$$
$$3241 \quad 3412 \quad 1423 \quad 2143$$
$$3214 \quad 3421 \quad 4123 \quad 1243$$

This method is known as "hunting the treble up and down," and was invented by Fabian Stedman, a Cambridge printer, who printed in 1667 the earliest treatise on change-ringing. If the above table is carefully observed, it will be seen that the first bell, or treble, shifts its place by one each time, backwards or forwards, while the other three only change six times in all; in other words, if the treble was omitted it would be a peal of six changes on three bells.

When we come to rings of five, six, or eight bells, these changes are, of course, capable of greater variety. On five bells we may have 5 times 24, or 120 changes; on six, 6 times 120, or 720; on eight bells, 40,320; and so on. But in actual practice it is very rare to have more than five or six thousand rung, even if there are eight or more bells; about 1,600 changes can be rung in the course of an hour, and two to three hours' consecutive work is as much as an ordinary ringer is capable of accomplishing. The essential feature of each set of changes is to bring the bells round to the order in which they started; as they would naturally do in the peal given above.

Plate 18.

The tenor bell of Exeter Cathedral, called "Grandison."
Recast by Taylor, 1902.

(See page 20.)

The result of the introduction of systematic and organized change-ringing was that companies or societies of ringers were very soon formed. So early as 1603 we hear of a company known as the "Scholars of Cheapside," formed in London. In 1637 was founded a famous London Society, that of the "College Youths," probably a revival of the one just named; its name is derived from some connection with Sir Richard Whittington's College of the Holy Ghost, near Cannon Street. It was to them that Stedman dedicated his *Tintinnalogia*, the work already mentioned. There is still an energetic "Ancient Society of College Youths," but it is not certain whether it can trace an actual descent from the older society. Another well-known ringing society is that of the "Cumberland Youths," originally "London Scholars," who changed their name in 1746 in compliment to the victor of Culloden.

Before leaving the subject, may I venture here a protest against the absurdities perpetrated by the artists of Christmas cards and illustrated magazines, in the attempt to render the form of a bell and the method in which it is rung? It is certain that few can ever have visited either belfry or ringing-chamber! Plate 29 gives a more truthful rendering of the method of ringing.

It may be fairly claimed as one of the far-reaching effects of the Church Revival that the conditions of our belfries and the conduct of our ringers will compare very favourably with what it was some forty or fifty years ago. Where the more accessible portions of the fabric were given over to dirt and neglect, and slovenliness was the chief feature of all ordinary forms of worship, it was hardly surprising that the towers and their internal arrangements were neglected, and frequently given over to more secular uses.

Nor was this merely a result of the general laxity and indifference of the "dead" period in the Church. There are not wanting signs that in the seventeenth century the standard of discipline among ringers was not high. We may recall how John Bunyan, at one time an enthusiastic member of the ringing company of Elstow, was constrained to abandon the pursuit, along with other enjoyments, as not tending to edification. That conviviality reigned in the belfry in those days is shown by the use of ringers' jugs, some of which still exist, in which large quantities of beer were provided, and by the frequent entries in parish accounts of money spent on beer for the ringers. One of the bells at Walsgrave, in Warwickshire (dated 1702) has the inscription:

> "Hark do you hear?
> Our clappers want beer,"

evidently intended for a gentle hint that the ringers suffered from thirst!

"Great John of Beverley."

A fourteenth-century bell recast by Taylor, with old lettering reproduced.

(See pages 22, 54, 73.)

At the same time there was a feeling that the actual ringing should be properly carried out, which finds vent in the numerous "Ringers' Rules," mostly dating from the eighteenth century, which may be seen painted up on the walls of our belfries. They all follow very much on one pattern, and one of the best versions is at Tong, in Shropshire, which may be given as an example—

> "If that to Ring you doe come here
> You must ring well with hand and eare.
> Keep stroak of time and goe not out;
> Or else you forfeit out of doubt.
> Our law is so concluded here
> For every fault a jugg of beer.
> If that you Ring with Spurr or Hat
> A jugg of beer must pay for that.
> If that you take a Rope in hand,
> These forfeits you must understand.
> Or if that you a Bell ou'r-throw
> It must cost Sixpence e're you goe.
> If in this place you sweare or curse,
> Sixpence to pay, pull out your purse:
> Come pay the Clerk, it is his fee;
> For one that Swears shall not goe free.
> These laws are Old, and are not new;
> Therefore the Clerk must have his due."

GEO. HARRISON, 1694.

It is satisfactory to note that the rule against swearing was very generally included, though possibly honoured more in the breach than the observance; but it is probable that the objection to wearing a hat was more on the grounds of inconvenience to the ringers than of irreverence.

As late as 1857, the Rev. W. C. Lukis, one of the earliest writers on church bells, complained of his own county, Wiltshire, that "there are sets of men who ring for what they can get, which they consume in drink; but there is very little love for the science or its music; and alas! much irreverence and profanation of the House of GOD. There is no 'plucking at the bells' for recreation and exercise. Church-ringers with us have degenerated into mercenary performers. In more than one parish where there are beautiful bells, I was told that the village youths took no interest whatever in bell-ringing, and had no desire to enter upon change-ringing."

Although less money is available nowadays for payments to ringers on special occasions, it may be feared that these remarks still hold good to some extent. But in other respects there is undoubted improvement. We do not now hear of "prize-ringing," or ringing in celebration of a victory in the Derby or in a parliamentary election, and if our ringing-chambers do not always reach a high standard of decency, there is a marked improvement in the character and behaviour of the ringers themselves.

CHAPTER V

USES AND CUSTOMS OF BELLS

An old monkish rhyme sums up the ancient uses of bells as follows:—

> "Laudo Deum verum, plebem voco, congrego clerum;
> Defunctos ploro, pestem fugo, festa decoro;
> Funera plango, fulgura frango, sabbata pango;
> Excito lentos, dissipo ventos, paco cruentos":

which may be rendered in English:—

> "I praise the true God, I call the people, I assemble the clergy;
> I mourn the departed, I put to flight pestilence, I honour festivals;
> I knoll for burials, I break the power of the lightning, I mark the sabbaths;
> I rouse the sluggard, I disperse the winds, I calm the bloodthirsty."

These lines will be familiar to readers of Longfellow's *Golden Legend*; but some of the uses mentioned belong to a time when bells were thought to have a magic power over the forces of nature, and a category of modern uses embraces many others here ignored.

The modern uses of bells naturally fall into two main divisions—religious and secular, or quasi-religious uses. By the former I mean the ringing of bells for divine service, and, in particular, for the festivals of the Church, and their use at weddings, funerals, and other events of life with which the Church is naturally concerned. Other uses, again, though now purely secular, had once a religious meaning, such as the Curfew and Pancake bells. More secular uses are those of the Gleaning bell and the Fire bell, of bells rung for local meetings or festivities, or in commemoration of national events.

The only allusion to bells in our Prayer Book is in the Preface, which directs that the minister "shall cause a bell to be tolled thereunto a convenient time before he begin, that the people may come to hear Goᴅ's Word, and to pray with him." This was, of course, the original purpose for which bells were applied to an ecclesiastical use, and by virtue of which they are reckoned among the "Ornaments of the Church." It is, therefore, the rule that every place of worship within the realm of the Church should have at least one bell, and in England at any rate there are not more than half a dozen parishes where the rule is ignored. The fifteenth Canon similarly enjoins the ringing of a bell on Wednesdays and Fridays for the Litany.

Plate 20.

The great bell of Tong Church, Shropshire.
Recast by Taylor, 1892.

(See page 22.)

Methods of ringing the bells for service depend largely on the number of bells available and the possibility of collecting ringers together; and the ringing of peals at these times is comparatively rare. Ordinarily, where there are more than two, the bells are chimed for periods varying from ten minutes to half an hour on Sundays, while on week-days a single bell perforce suffices, tolled haply by the parson himself. In many places it is the custom to toll the largest bell for the last few minutes before service begins; this is known as the "Sermon Bell," and was originally meant to indicate that a sermon would be preached. Or the smallest bell is rung hurriedly, as if to warn laggards, and this is called the "ting-tang," "priest's," or "parson's" bell. Some of these little bells bear the appropriate inscription, "Come away make no delay." The use of a sermon bell is said to date from before the Reformation.

In many parishes it used to be an invariable custom to ring a single bell, or chime several, at eight o'clock on Sunday morning; this, however, has lost its original significance since the general introduction of early Celebrations. In former times the regular hour for Mattins was at eight, followed by Mass at the canonical hour of nine, and though such an arrangement of services soon came to an end after the Reformation, the bells which used to announce them were continued even down to the present day. There are still not a few parishes where a bell is rung at nine as well as at eight, even when there are no early services.

In pre-Reformation days most churches possessed, besides the regular "ring," several smaller bells, which are described in inventories as "saunce" or "sanctus" bells, "sacring bells," and so on. Their uses are sometimes confused nowadays, but were clearly defined. The sanctus bell, or saunce, usually hung in a turret or cot on the gable over the chancel arch, and was intended to announce the progress of the service to those outside who could not come to church. It was rung at that point in the Sarum or English rites of the Eucharist when the singing of the *Sanctus* or "Holy, Holy, Holy," just before the Canon of the Mass, was reached; whence its name. The sacring-bell, on the other hand, was much smaller, and hung *inside* the church, usually on the rood-screen. It was rung at the end of the Consecration Prayer, or "prayer of sacring" (Plate 30), and announced the completion of the act of sacrifice. The Reformers made a dead set against these practices, but it is difficult to see that much superstition was involved therein, and the revival in modern days of the "sacring bell" in the form of a few strokes at the time of the consecration has more to recommend than to condemn it.

A few sacring bells still exist, hanging on rood-screens, in East Anglian churches, as at Salhouse and Scarning (Plate 31), and one at Yelverton, in Norfolk, has just been restored to its old position. Ancient sanctus bells are more numerous, and a few still hang in their original cots, as at Wrington, in Somerset, and Idbury, in Oxfordshire (Plate 32). They have mostly been fixed in the towers and used as "ting-tangs." The majority have no inscription on them, but there are notable exceptions in some of the Midland counties.

"Great Paul."

Cast by Taylor, 1881. Now hanging in the south-west tower of
S. Paul's Cathedral.

(See page 25.)

The only other "Sunday use" to which I have to draw attention is the ringing of a bell *after* services. This is, or was, sometimes done with the object of notifying a service in the afternoon; but it is known in some places, as at Mistley, in Essex, as the "Pudding Bell," it being supposed that it was intended to warn housewives to get ready the Sunday dinner! Some writers have thought that this midday bell is really a survival of the midday *Angelus*, or *Ave* bell; but it is more likely to date from the bad times of non-residence and irregular services.

The ringing of bells on festivals is more particularly associated with Christmas and the New Year, though the latter is a secular rather than a religious occasion. The Christmas bells have been a favourite theme with poets, great and small, and the best-known lines on the subject are in Tennyson's *In Memoriam*, said to have been composed by him on hearing the bells of Waltham Abbey, in Essex (Plate 33).

> "The time draws near the birth of Christ;
> The moon is hid; the night is still;
> The Christmas bells from hill to hill
> Answer each other in the mist."

And again:

> "The time draws near the birth of Christ;
> The moon is hid, the night is still;
> A single church below the hill
> Is pealing, folded in the mist."

The more famous stanzas, beginning:

> "Ring out, wild bells, to the wild sky,
> The flying cloud, the frosty light:
> The year is dying in the night;
> Ring out, wild bells and let him die.
>
> Ring out the old, ring in the new,
> Ring, happy bells, across the snow;
> The year is going, let him go;
> Ring out the false, ring in the true,"

refer rather to New Year's Eve.

On New Year's Eve the old year is rung out and the new year in, in many parishes. Sometimes one bell only is tolled until the clock strikes twelve, in other cases the bells are rung muffled, i.e., with the clappers wrapped round to deaden the sound, these being uncovered at midnight, when a merry "open" peal bursts forth. Either practice is to be preferred to that of ringing consecutively before and after the hour, which obscures the significance of the performance.

A muffled peal is sometimes rung on the Holy Innocents' Day, a custom said to be kept up still in Herefordshire; and in addition to the Greater Festivals, the Epiphany, All Saints' Day, S. Andrew's Day, and S. Thomas's Day, have been or are still specially honoured. Ringing on the last-named occasion, which is kept up in several Warwickshire parishes, appears to be associated with the distribution of local charities. But ringing on "superstitious" occasions, not mentioned in the

Book of Common Prayer, is forbidden by the 88th Canon.

Plate 22.

The old "Great Tom" of Westminster.

Recast by Philip Wightman in 1698. From an old drawing, made before
its recasting by Phelps in 1716.

(See page 25.)

Another day of the Church's year with which bell-ringing is associated is
Shrove Tuesday, on which day the Pancake bell is rung in some places at eleven
o'clock. Two bells are generally used, the sound of which is supposed to resemble
the word "pancake." The origin of the custom is to be found in the calling of the
faithful to confess their sins and be "shriven" at the beginning of the Lenten fast.
That pancakes were associated with this day is due to the fact that butter was
forbidden during the whole of Lent. It was always the Church's rule that the bells
should be silent during that season—at least that there should be no peal-ringing
in Lent, and no bells used at all during Holy Week; and this is now generally observed.

Plate 23.

The Belfry of Bruges.

(See page 29.)

Except in the case of royalty we seldom now hear of bells being rung to usher mankind into the world; but they have always been associated with the rejoicings of a wedding ceremony, and in some parts, as in Lincolnshire, are even rung at the putting up of Banns. But their use at the time of death is even more universal.

The passing bell originally sounded as a summons to the faithful to pray for a soul just passing out of the world; but it has now degenerated into a mere notice that death has taken place, and as it is rung (to suit the sexton's convenience) some hours after death, or even on the following day, the name has ceased to be appropriate. It appears to be one of the oldest of all uses of bells, and is said to have been rung for S. Hilda, of Whitby, in 680. Unlike most other customs it received the strong approval of the most ardent reformers, and in the churchwardens' accounts of the sixteenth and seventeenth centuries there are often long lists given every year of money received from parishioners "for the Knell." The sum paid was usually fourpence. The 67th Canon directs that the passing bell shall be tolled, "and the minister shall not then slack to do his last duty."

When the Knell is rung, it is a frequent practice to indicate the age or sex of the deceased. The former is done by tolling a number of strokes answering to the years of his or her life, or more vaguely by using the largest bell for an adult and a smaller for a child. Sex is sometimes similarly indicated, but more usually by what are known as "tellers," a varying number of strokes for male or female, and sometimes also for a child. The commonest form is three times three for male, three times two for female; and sometimes three times singly for a child; but some parishes keep up curious variations of this rule. The old saying "nine tailors make a man" is really "nine tellers," or three times three.

The knell with the tellers is sometimes repeated at funerals, but more frequently the tenor bell is tolled at intervals of a minute, becoming more rapid when the corpse appears in sight. In some country districts the bells are or used to be chimed at this time, and in Shropshire this is known as the "joy-bells," or "ringing the dead home." In olden days a hand-bell or "lych-bell" was rung before the corpse on its way; this is still done at Oxford at the funeral of any University official.

Bells were largely used in mediaeval times to mark the hours of the day, even before the introduction of clocks. In the monastic establishments they were naturally rung at the canonical hours of twelve, three, six, and nine, for the services of Mattins, Lauds, Prime, Tierce, Sext, None, Vespers, and Compline. It has been suggested that this is the reason why chimes are usually played at these hours, where there are carillons.

But one of the best known uses of bells for this purpose is the Curfew, which was often accompanied by a corresponding bell in the early morning. We have usually been taught that the Curfew or "cover-fire" was a tyrannical and unpopular enactment by William the Conqueror, and therefore a purely legal and secular institution. There is, however, evidence that it was in use long before at Oxford, where King Alfred directed that it should be rung every evening (as it is still); and William probably only made use of an existing custom for the beneficent purpose of guarding against fires.

Photo by]   [*J. Valentine & Sons.*

The Campanile or Bell-Tower of Chichester Cathedral.

(See page 29.)

But it has also been suggested that the Curfew was in its origin a bell with a religious as well as a secular significance, namely the Ave bell, or Angelus, which was rung in the early morning and the evening, usually at 9 a.m. and 5.30 p.m., and also at midday, and at the sound of which every one was expected to repeat the memorial of the Incarnation or "Hail Mary." Some have thought that bells dedicated to the angel Gabriel were specially devoted to such a purpose; but this is doubtful, though the old Curfew bell at S. Albans still bears such a dedication. At Mexborough, in Yorkshire, a bell is rung morning, noon, and evening, obviously a survival of the Angelus bell.

The Curfew bell seems to have appealed especially to poets, even to the American Longfellow, and the puritan Milton, who in *Il Penseroso* says:

> "Oft on a plat of rising ground
> I hear the far-off Curfew sound
> Over some wide-watered shore
> Swinging slow with sullen roar."

Compare the opening line of Gray's *Elegy*:

> "The curfew tolls the knell of parting day."

The morning bell, whether an Ave bell or not, is seldom now rung, but may be heard at 5 a.m. at Ludlow, and at Nuneaton and Coleshill in Warwickshire. One of the old bells of S. Michael's, Coventry, now at S. John's Church in that town, has the inscription:

> "I ring at six to let men know
> When to and from their work to go. 1675."

The Curfew bell, though alas! growing rapidly rarer, may be heard at 9 p.m. all the year round in our two University towns; and is also rung at eight at Ludlow, Pershore, Shrewsbury, and in Warwickshire. But it is now usually confined to the winter months, from Michaelmas to Lady Day, or an even shorter period. In some places the day of the month is tolled afterwards, as at Cambridge; at Oxford 101 strokes are given, representing the number of persons on the foundation of Christ Church.

Of purely secular uses of bells space forbids me to say much. The Gleaning bell used to be rung in many parishes during harvest, morning and evening, to signify to the people when gleaning was allowed. With the decay of agriculture in England this use has almost died out, especially in the midlands, but it is still kept up in corn-growing parts, as in the north of Essex.

Ringing has always been customary—at least since the Reformation—on secular anniversaries, such as the birthday or Coronation Day of the Sovereign, or on the occasion of great victories. It was also very common at one time on Restoration Day (May 29th), and Gunpowder Plot Day (November 5th), but—perhaps since their removal from our Prayer Book—these occasions are becoming more and more ignored. Ringing on November 5th is, however, still common in Warwickshire. Another day on which ringing was often practised was that of the parish feast, usually corresponding with the patronal festival, or day on which the original dedication of the church was honoured.

Plate 25.

The old Campanile of King's College, Cambridge.
Destroyed in the eighteenth century. It contained five large bells.

(See page 29.)

It is or has been a tradition in some places that in cases of fire the church bells should be rung backwards; and elsewhere a bell was specially devoted to this purpose. At S. Mary's, Warwick, there is a small fire bell dated 1670, which, however, is not now hung; and there is a well-known one at Sherborne, in Dorset, dated 1653, with the inscription:

> "Lord, quench the furious flame;
> Arise, run, help, put out the same."

The large and small bells of the Guild Chapel, Stratford-on-Avon, are also intended to be rung in cases of fire.

The ringing of daily bells, especially at night, is often accounted for by stories of people who found their way when lost, or were delivered from nocturnal dangers, by hearing the bell of some church. Instances of this are scattered all over the country, and there are the Ashburnham bell at Chelsea, the great bell of Tong in Shropshire, and others which were originally given in commemoration of such events, with the object of keeping up the ringing for the benefit of other wanderers.

CHAPTER VI
THE DECORATION OF BELLS
AND THEIR INSCRIPTIONS

Most of us are probably aware that it is usual for bells to bear inscriptions, be it only the date or name of the maker; but few who have not actually examined bells for themselves may have discovered that they are often richly or effectively decorated. We do not as a rule find them as highly ornamented as foreign bells, which often have every available space covered with inscriptions, figures and devices, or borders of ornament; but to some the greater soberness of the English method may seem preferable. Nor is this practice of ornamenting bells confined to the more artistic age before the Reformation. Some of our most richly decorated bells belong to the seventeenth century or even later (see Plate 38); and it is only the character of the ornamentation which is changed.

In point of fact the earliest bells are usually the plainest, and the mediaeval craftsman contented himself with devoting his skill to producing elegant and artistic lettering, beautiful initial crosses, or ingenious foundry marks (Plates 14, 36). The latter were introduced about the end of the fourteenth century, when, as we have seen in an earlier chapter, the guild of braziers or "belleyeteres" were more regularly organized. Those used by Henry Jordan (see page 13) are good examples; as are the shields of the Bury and Norwich foundries (page 13). In the West and North of England such devices are rarer; but badges, such as the Bristol ship, or the Worcester "Royal Heads," take their place. One or two of the London founders use the symbols of the four Evangelists (Plate 34). A favourite device is the merchant's mark, a kind of monogram, or the rebus, a pictorial pun on the founder's name. John Tonne, who worked in Sussex and Essex about 1520–1540, decorated his bells in the French fashion, with large florid crosses, busts and figures, and other devices (Plate 35).

Initial crosses are almost invariably found on mediaeval bells, and their variety is endless, from the plainest form of Greek cross to the elaborate specimen shown on Plate 36, which is found in the Midland counties. The words were frequently divided by stops, varying from a simple row of three dots ⦂ to such devices as a wheel, a rosette, or an ornamented oblong panel. Impressions from coins pressed into the mould are by no means uncommon.

The "Bell House" in the Churchyard at East Bergholt, Suffolk.

(See page 29.)

But often the chief or sole beauty of a mediaeval bell is its lettering. In the fourteenth century this is invariably composed of capital letters throughout, of the ornamental form known as Gothic or Lombardic (Plate 36). Towards the end of that century the black-letter text used in manuscripts was introduced into other branches of art, such as brasses, and thus also makes its appearance on bells. But the initial letter of each word is still executed in the old Gothic capitals, and such inscriptions are known as "Mixed Gothic" (Plate 37), later ones of the sixteenth century being more strictly styled "black-letter," where no capitals are used. The change, however, was not universal, and many of the foundries in the West and North of England preferred to adhere to the capitals down to the Reformation; while even in London, as at Leicester, Reading, and elsewhere, there was a distinct revival of inscriptions in capitals during the sixteenth century.

Plate 27.

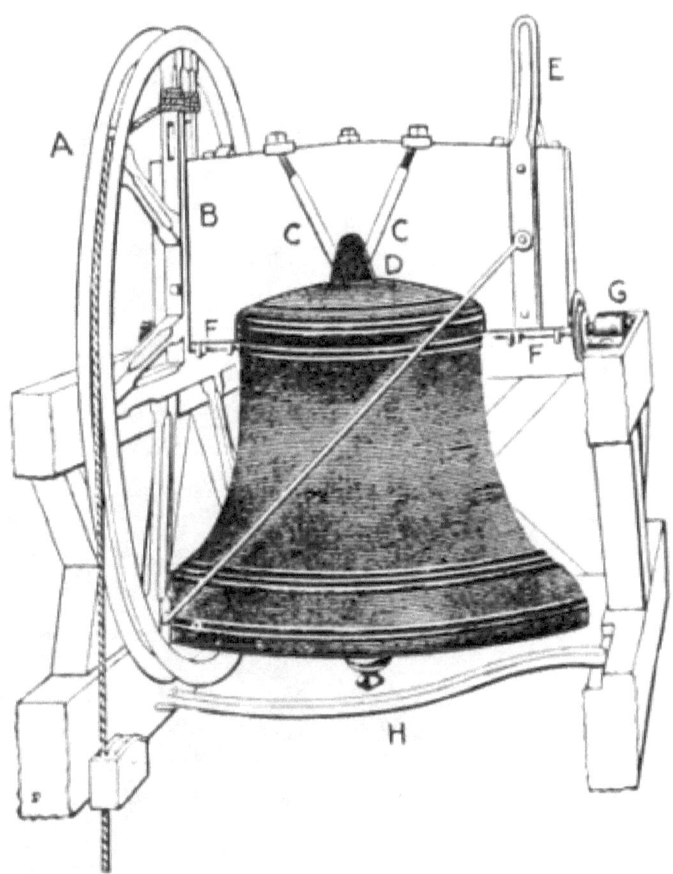

Diagram showing method of hanging a bell for ringing

(see page 31.)

A.   Wheel with rope attached.   E.   Stay.

B.   Headstock.   FF.   Gudgeons.

CC.   Straps or Keys.   G.   Brasses (in which the gudgeons revolve).

D.   Cannons (modern form).   H.   Slider.

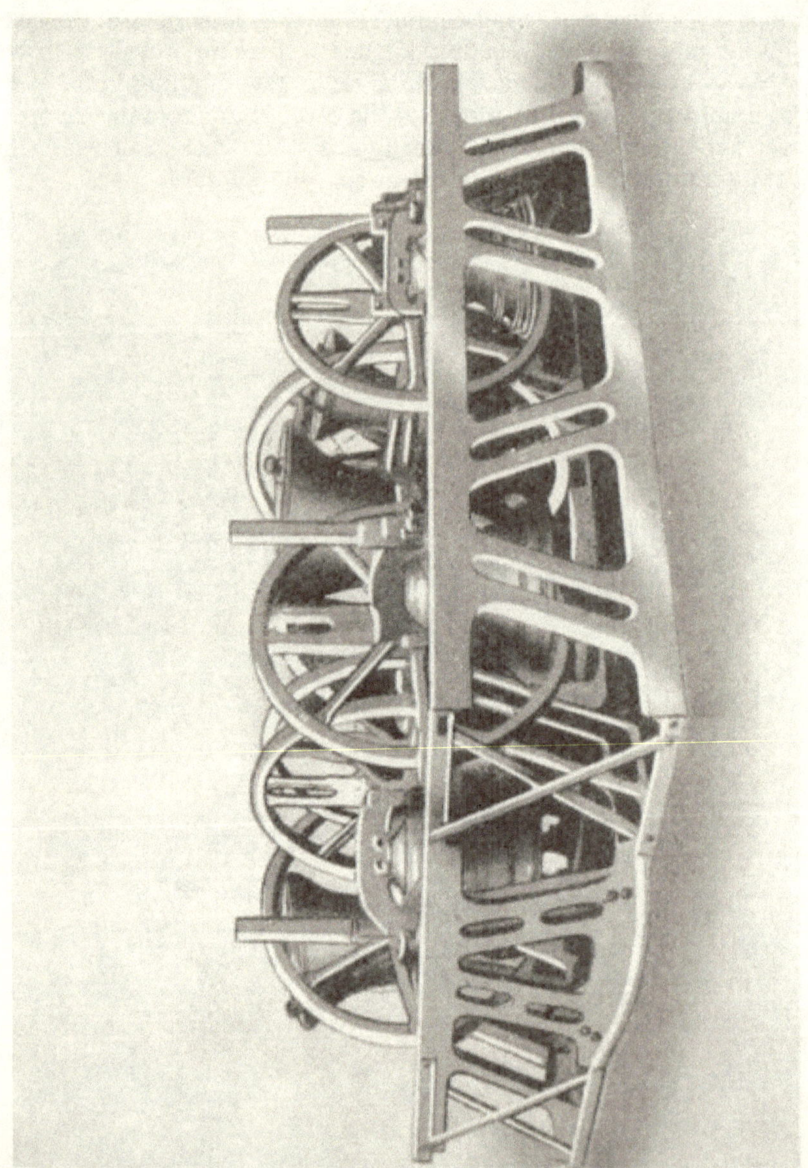

Peal of Eight Bells (Tenor 16 cwt.) for Aberavon Church, Glamorganshire.

This is an example of an ordinary English peal constructed for change-ringing and shows some of the bells "up," ready for ringing. In this case the frame and stocks are of iron and the bells are without cannons.

The reign of Queen Elizabeth is usually regarded as a period of transition, and there was, before the general introduction of modern Roman lettering, a time when no general rule was observed. Some founders used Gothic capitals; others black-letter; others again, nondescript ornate capitals difficult to classify; while the Roman lettering, introduced about 1560–70, gradually ousted all the older styles from favour, and with very few exceptions became general about 1620. The use of older lettering and stamps by many founders during this "transition" period is noteworthy. The Leicester founders were especially addicted to this practice, and among other old stamps bought up the beautiful lettering and ornaments used by the Brasyers, of Norwich, in the fifteenth century. Henry Oldfield of Nottingham (1580–1620), and Robert Mot of London (1575–1608), may also be mentioned under this head.

I have said that seventeenth century bells were often very richly decorated; and the ornamental running borders or elaborate arabesque patterns which separate the words of the inscriptions or surround the upper and lower edges of the bells, surpass in that respect anything attempted in mediaeval times (Plate 38). Thomas Hancox of Walsall (1620–1640) adorned his bells with reproductions of mediaeval seals; and as late as the beginning of the eighteenth century the Cors of Aldbourne, in Wiltshire, bought up a lot of pieces of old brass ornaments from which they used to decorate their bells. At Malmesbury and Tisbury in that county they have left bells covered with figures of cherubs, coats of arms and monograms, a medallion of the Adoration of the Wise Men, and other curious ornaments. Most of these founders, such as John Martin of Worcester, Oldfield of Nottingham, and Clibury of Wellington, used trade-marks with their initials, and a bell or other device.

Seventeenth-century Roman lettering, although plain, is often most effective and artistic; capitals are almost always used throughout, and small Roman letters are very rare. It is not until the middle of the next century that it was replaced by the dull mechanical printing types which are characteristic of the present day. But since the Gothic revival several modern founders have re-introduced capital letters of the old style with good effect; notably the Taylors of Loughborough. Nowadays, however, there is little attempt at ornamenting bells; not only the usual inscription-band on the shoulder, but the whole surface of the bell is utilized for immortalizing local officials and celebrities. On a bell recently cast for a church on the outskirts of London are given the names, not only of the Vicar, Bishop, and Archbishop, but of the Prime Minister, Member of Parliament, and Chairman of the District Council!

So far little has been said about the inscriptions placed on bells; but as these form one of the most interesting features of the subject, they demand some little attention.

The earliest inscriptions, those of the fourteenth century, were usually in Latin, and very simple in form. We find merely a name such as IESVS or IOHANNES, or such phrases as CAMPANA BEATI PAVLI, "the bell of blessed Paul," or IN HONORE SANCTI LAURENCII, "in honour of Saint Lawrence." More rarely, the founder's name, as—

MICHAEL DE VVYMBIS ME FECIT
"Michael de Wymbis made me."

𝕴𝕺𝕹 𝕸𝕰 𝖄𝕰𝖄𝕿
"John cast me."

Other forms of inscription soon became common, especially the simple invocation to a saint—

"Sancte Petre (or 'Sancta Katerina') ora pro nobis."
"Saint Peter," or "Saint Katherine, pray for us."

By one founder, whose theology was somewhat confused, the Holy Trinity itself was similarly invoked—

"Sancta Trinitas ora pro nobis."

He should have said "miserere nobis," "have mercy upon us," as in our Litany.

What are known as "leonines," or rhyming hexameter verses, are also very popular, such as—

IN MULTIS ANNIS RESONET CAMPANA IOHANNIS
"For many years let the bell of John resound."

VIRGINIS EGREGIE VOCOR CAMPANA MARIE
"I am called the bell of Mary the excellent Virgin."

MISSI DE CELIS HABEO NOMEN GABRIELIS
"I have the name of heaven-sent Gabriel."

VIRGO CORONATA DUC NOS AD REGNA BEATA
"Crowned Virgin, lead us to realms of bliss."

SUM ROSA PULSATA MUNDI KATERINA VOCATA
"I am the rose of the world, when struck, called Katherine."

Most frequent of all is the Angelic salutation (*S. Luke* i. 28):

AVE MARIA GRACIA PLENA DOMINUS TECUM

sometimes found in an English form as—

"HAIL MARY FUL OF GRAS"
("Full of grace").

There are said to be altogether seventy different forms of dedication to the Blessed Virgin. She is by far the favourite saint with bell-founders, though S. Katherine (possibly on account of her emblem the wheel) was their special patron. On the whole the dedications correspond fairly to those favoured for churches; but we note that S. Andrew, S. James, and S. Paul, are rarely found, whereas S. Anne and S. Gabriel are more common. We must not expect to find bells necessarily dedicated to the patron saints of their churches; it is in fact exceptional, and possibly the name was determined by that of some guild or chantry. Where they are the same it is usually the tenor; but the old ring of five at S. Bartholomew, Smithfield, has the treble dedicated to that saint.

Plate 29.

**Ringers at S. Paul's Cathedral Ringing a Peal on New Year's
Eve on the Twelve Bells.**

(See page 34.)

Among texts of scripture are also found

SIT NOMEN DOMINI BENEDICTUM
"Blessed be the Name of the Lord" (*Job* i. 21).

IESVS NAZARENVS REX IVDEORVM
"Jesus of Nazareth the King of the Jews"
(*S. John* xix. 19).

BEATVS VENTER QVI TE PORTAVIT
"Blessed is the womb that bare thee" (*S. Luke* xi. 27).

But such texts become commoner in the seventeenth century. An early post-Reformation example is at Hannington, Northants:

LOVE HORTETH NOT (*Rom.* xiii. 10).

Sometimes a bell bears a prayer for its donor, or for his soul, as at Goring, Oxfordshire—

ORATE PRO PETRO EXONIENSE EPISCOPO,
"Pray for Peter, Bishop of Exeter."

This was Peter Quivil, Bishop about 1290. Or at Bolton-in-Craven, Yorkshire—

Sc'e Paule, ora pro a'i'abus Henrici Pudsey et Margarete consorte sue
"St. Paul, pray for the souls of Henry Pudsey and Margaret his wife."

In these cases we are enabled to gain a clue to the date of the bell, a piece of information rarely found given in mediaeval times. Henry Pudsey, for instance, died about 1510. There is an interesting bell at Aldbourne, in Wiltshire, dated 1516, with a prayer for the souls of Richard Goddard of Upham, his two wives and his children. It is said that this is the only known record of his double marriage, though the family is an old one, well known in those parts.

English inscriptions are very rare, but when found are often very quaint, as at Snowshill, in Gloucestershire—

"IN NAME OF TRINITE; GILLIS [Giles'] BELLE MEN CALLE ME";

or at Alkborough, in Lincolnshire—

"JESU FOR YI MODIR [the Mother's] SAKE SAVE AL YE SAULS
THAT ME GART MAKE [had made] AMEN."

The Reformation brought about a great, though not an immediate but gradual, change in the character of bell inscriptions. We often find about this time the whole or a portion of the alphabet; and it has been supposed that the founder wished to use his old stamps, but was afraid of giving offence by adhering to the old style of inscription, and so arranged the letters in a fashion to which none could object! But right through the Reformation period, the reign of Elizabeth, and the ensuing Stuart period, it is by no means rare to find the old formulae repeated. It is possible that ignorant founders reproduced them when recasting bells, without realizing their meaning, or that they trusted to the inaccessibility of belfries, not to be found out! Still the fact remains, not only that more "Popish" inscriptions were left intact by Reformer and Puritan on bells than on any other part of the fabric of churches, but also that prejudice and fanaticism here seems to have played a smaller part. Yet there are indications of Protestant zeal on the part of some seventeenth-century founders. Tobie Norris of Stamford (1603–1626) is fond of proclaiming—

NON SONO ANIMABVS MORTVORVM SED AVRIBVS VIVENTIVM
"I sound not for the souls of the dead but for the ears of the living";

and William Purdue of Bristol, in 1678, perhaps with the fear of James II's advent to the throne before his eyes, gives vent to the prayer:

LORD BY THY MIGHT KEEP US FROM POOPE AND HYPOCRITE,

at Stanley S. Leonard, Gloucestershire.

Plate 30.

The Ringing of the Sacring Bell by a Clerk in Minor Orders.

From a Manuscript in the British Museum.

(*See pages 31, 39.*)

For the most part the inscriptions of this period are, when not merely church-wardens' names, coloured with a piety which finds vent in quaint and homely expressions, such as "FEARE GOD," "IESVS BEE OVR SPEED," "IN GOD IS MY HOPE." They remind us of the bells of Rylstone, in Yorkshire, of which Wordsworth says:

> "When the bells of Rylstone played
> Their Sabbath music—*God us ayde*—
> Inscriptive legend, which I ween,
> May on those holy bells be seen."

He was, however, unfortunately misinformed, as the true inscription (on one bell) was, "In God is all." Other attempts are more ambitious, such as—

I AM A CRIER IN THE HOUSE OF GOD COME AND KIP [keep] HOLI,

at Witcomb, Gloucestershire (1630), or—

BE MECKE AND LOLY TO HEARE THE WORD OF GOD,

at Chichester Cathedral (1587). Some of these inscriptions are on bells by John Wallis of Salisbury, of whom it has been said, "If we estimate him by his works he was a great man; and if we take his laconic epigraphs as an index of his heart, he was a trustful, thankful, religious character." They are, at all events, characteristic of the sober and straightforward piety of the days of George Herbert and Bishop Andrewes. Three more characteristic expressions of the period are largely used by the Nottingham founders:

> "I sweetly toling men do call to taste on meate that feeds the soule."

> "All you who hear my roaring sound repent before you lie in ground."

> "My roaring sound doth warning give that men may not here always live."

Other founders, like Tobie Norris, already quoted, preferred to use Latin. Another favourite of his is—

NON CLAMOR SED AMOR CANTAT IN AVRE DEI

"The sound that reacheth God above
Is not a clang but voice of love."

A very beautiful Latin inscription, and most remarkable for the time when it was composed (1651), is on the tenor at Stockton, Salop; it runs in English—

> "Glory in the highest to God the Father, Son, and Holy Ghost; William Whitmore, Knight, patron and restorer of this church, now called to the Church triumphant, vowed and designed me for the use of the Church militant."

Plate 31.

Sacring Bell hung on Rood-Screen, Scarning Church, Norfolk.

(See page 39.)

More quaint than edifying are the following, found at Thatcham in Berkshire —

    1. I AS TREBIL BEGIN
    2. I AS SECOND WIL SING
    3. I AS THIRD WIL RING
    4. I AS FORTH IN MY PLACE
    5. I AS FIFT WILL SOVND
    6. I AS TENNAR HVM ALL ROVND.

We pass from these to others of the same period, which show a sad falling-off in poetry and sentiment. Early in the seventeenth century the deplorable habit of self-advertisement was begun by the Newcombes of Leicester, who invented the distich —

    BE YT KNOWNE TO ALL THAT DOTH ME SEE
    THAT NEWCOMBE OF LEICESTER MADE ME.

This is adopted, but not improved, by later founders, as by Henry Farmer of Gloucester, who, on a bell of 1623, at Throckmorton, in Worcestershire, proclaims —

    BE IT KNOWNE TO ALL THAT SHALL VS SEE
    THAT HENRIE FARMER MADE WE 4 OF 3.

Worse depths are reached by Richard Keene of Woodstock on two bells at Brailes, Warwickshire. On one is —

    IME NOT THE BELL I WAS BUT QUITE ANOTHER
    IME NOW AS RIGHT AND TRUE AS GEORGE MY BROTHER.

On the other —

    I'LL CRACK NO MORE NOW RING YOUR FILL
    MERRY GEORGE I WAS AND WILL BE STILL.

This style of inscription is even more characteristic of the early eighteenth century; and we find at Meriden, in Warwickshire —

    WHEN MY FIRST AND THIRD BEGIN TO RING
    MY THIRD WAS BROKE BEFORE WE ALL DID SING.

There is a pun here on the name of the founder, William Brooke. An even worse punster is Henry Pleasant of Sudbury, who at All Saints', Maldon, placed on four of the bells the following effusions —

    (1) WHEN THREE THIS STEEPLE FIRST DID HOLD
    (2) WE WERE THREE EMBLEMS OF A SCOLD
    (3) NO MUSICK THEN BUT NOW [YOU] SHALL SEE
    (4) WHAT *PLEASANT* MUSICK SIX WILL BE.

Joseph Smith of Edgbaston, another would-be poet, has several inscriptions of this class, as at Alvechurch, Worcestershire —

    IF YOU WOULD KNOW WHEN WE WARE RUNN
    IT WAS MARCH THE 22, 1711 [i.e., "seventeen-one-one"].

Plate 32.

Ancient Sanctus Bell (Fourteenth Century).

In its Original Cot over the Chancel Arch of Idbury Church, Oxfordshire.

(See page 39.)

Tower of Waltham Abbey Church, Essex.

The Bells of which inspired Tennyson's well-known lines.

(See page 41.)

Yet another type of vulgarity is to be found at Bakewell, Somerset—

BILBIE AND BOOSH MAY COME AND SEE
WHAT EVANS AND NOTT HAVE DONE FOR ME.

When we reach the middle of the century a change comes over the inscriptions, though hardly one for the better. The frivolous doggerel rhymes are replaced by prim, though not always decorous, couplets which seem to be thoroughly characteristic of that period. In fact, so greatly was Methodism feared by the correct and worldly churchmen of Georgian days that we actually find on a bell at Welwyn, Herts.—

PROSPERITY TO THE CHURCH OF ENGLAND
AND NO ENCOURAGEMENT TO ENTHUSIASM.

The most typical specimens, however, are on the bells of the London founders at this period—

AT PROPER TIMES OUR VOICES WE WILL RAISE
IN SOUNDING TO OUR BENEFACTORS' PRAISE.

WHEN FEMALE VIRTUE WEDS WITH MANLY WORTH
WE CATCH THE RAPTURE AND WE SPREAD IT FORTH

MAY ALL WHOM I SHALL SUMMON TO THE GRAVE
THE BLESSINGS OF A WELL-SPENT LIFE RECEIVE.

The last-named was composed by a Shropshire schoolmaster, who also devised verses of the same type for bells in his own church of High Ercall. One example may be given—

WHERE MEANDRING RODEN GENTLY GLIDES
OR TURNE'S PROUD CURRENT FILLS ITS AMPLE SIDES
HENCE MEDITATION VIEWS OUR CALM ABODE,
HEALS THE SICK MIND, AND YIELDS IT PURE TO GOD.

The Rudhalls of Gloucester, who were typical "Church and State" men, usually place on their tenor bells the familiar couplet—

I TO THE CHURCH THE LIVING CALL
AND TO THE GRAVE DO SUMMON ALL.

Perhaps the worst specimen of the taste of this period is to be found at Hornsey, in Middlesex—

THE RINGER'S ART OUR GRACEFUL NOTES PROLONG;
APOLLO LISTENS AND APPROVES THE SONG.

Doubtless this seemed appropriate enough to an age which adorned its tombs and churchyards with cupids, urns, and such-like pagan emblems.

Other examples of this kind from the provinces are—

THE PUBLIC RAISED ME WITH A LIBERAL HAND;
WE COME WITH HARMONY TO CHEER THE LAND [Stroud].

ALL YOU OF BATH THAT HEARE ME SOUND

THANK LADY HOPTON'S HUNDRED POUND [Bath Abbey].

Some inscriptions again are of historical interest, such as at Child Okeford, Dorset, where, in 1648,

GOD BLESS KING CHARLES

was actually placed on a bell by a founder who must have had the courage of his convictions! It need hardly be pointed out that the royal cause was just then at the depth of unpopularity. The eight bells of S. Helen's, Worcester, bear the names of Marlborough's victories in Queen Anne's reign, with an appropriate couplet in each case. Other bells, such as the great bell of Glasgow Cathedral, and the tenor of Stepney, London, record their own history from mediaeval times down to their latest re-casting.

A curious form of inscription found on seventeenth-century bells, and sometimes revived at the present day, is the chronogram, where the date is given by Roman letters of a larger size than the rest of the inscription, as at Clifton-on-Teme, Worcestershire—

HENrICVs IEFFREYS KENELMo DeVoVIt,

where the letters MDCLVVVIII in numerical order read as the date 1668.

It is one of the many debts that we owe to the Church Revival of the last century that such desecrations of our bells as quoted above are now a thing of the past. If our modern bells are often very dull affairs as regards their decoration or inscriptions, we can at least be thankful that profanity and frivolity have disappeared. Though as I have already noted, a tendency to self-advertisement is still too apparent, there has been a great change in the last fifty years, and the improvement in the choice of inscriptions is most marked. Those to whom such things are a concern have begun to realize that a bell is a vehicle of history, and that, therefore, its history should be duly recorded and preserved. But what is of far more importance, they have also learned to look upon it as an instrument destined for God's service—as one of the "Ornaments of the Church"—and therefore just as deserving of honour as any other furniture of God's house.

Plate 34.

Symbols of the Four Evangelists.

Used as stamps by London bell-founders of the fifteenth century.

(See page 49.)

CHAPTER VII
THE CARE OF BELLS

It has already been pointed out that our bells deserve to be treated with care and reverence as much as any other part of the church fabric, because they not only have their historic interest, but are closely connected with our acts of worship and religious rites. I wish, therefore, in my concluding chapter, to offer a few suggestions as to their proper treatment. And when we speak of the bells in this connection we must not forget the belfries also.

Some fifty years ago the Rev. W. C. Lukis, whom I have already had occasion to quote, called attention to the disgraceful condition of many Wiltshire belfries, in words which were by no means too strong for the occasion. He pointed out that the neglect of the bells not only led to their becoming useless, but also endangered the whole fabric of the tower, and eventually did mischief to the parishioners also, who either had to do without their bells or pay for the repairs. Many of the towers were in so dangerous a state that the bells were forbidden to be rung, and though this may have been partly due to the vibration caused by change-ringing, for which, of course, the towers were not originally built, the evils were, in his opinion, due much more to neglect on the part of the churchwardens, who were responsible for the care of the bells.

"Bells," he says, "require very constant attention to keep them in ringing order." Therefore it is not the use of the bells, not even change-ringing of the most violent description, which destroys the bells and endangers the belfries; but simply neglect or carelessness. It must be borne in mind that bells are enormously heavy, and are yet required to move and revolve with perfect ease, and to be hung with perfect balance and adjustment of all their parts. Any temporary or amateurish repairs will probably end in doing more harm than good; nor will an occasional use of oil or new ropes supply all that is wanted. Above all, the frame-work must be kept clear of the walls of the tower, or the vibration will inevitably destroy it.

There is another matter to which the same writer calls attention, which, if not a source of danger to the bells, may often be so to those who visit them, and which in any case is a disgrace to those who have the House of God in their care. I allude to the condition of the staircases or ladders by which the bells are approached. "Generally speaking," says Mr. Lukis, "the dark, winding stone staircases (when they have any) leading to them are dirty, worn, and difficult to tread; and when you have secured your footing, you suddenly come upon a huge heap of sticks, straws, feathers, and other rubbish, the patient and laborious work of indefatigable jackdaws. When the towers have no stone staircases, the bells have to be reached by a succession of crazy ladders, planted on equally crazy floors. Why should towers be so desecrated? Are they not as much a portion of the church as any other part?"

Plate 35.

Bell by John Tonne, a Founder of Henry VIII's time (1520–1540). Ornamented in the French fashion.

(See page 49.)

Specimens of Gothic capital letters.

Both sets are reduced to about half size.

(*See pages 15, 22, 50.*)

These words, at the time they were written, were doubtless true of the majority of belfries in the country; but I fear there are still not a few of which the same may be said. I have been into many a belfry, in which, on raising the trap-door admitting me to the bells, I have been forcibly convinced, by the showers of accumulated filth descending upon me, that they have literally not been visited for years! In justice it may be said that where proper access to the bells exists this is seldom the case. At the worst, the bottom of the staircase is made the receptacle for brushes, dust-pans, and candlesticks, or such-like necessary articles. But why should not proper access be provided in *every* case? Even the solitary tinkler in a small and elevated turret sometimes requires attention; and even if the casual visitor to a belfry must not always expect to be considered, it is surely reasonable that the parish official whose duty it is to care for the bells should not find obstacles placed in the way of reaching them. There are very few churches, not reckoning those where the bells are hung outside, in which a permanent ladder might not be fixed, where there is no possibility of a staircase. And this, whether of wood or iron, need not be either an expensive or unsightly object; but it should be stout and sound if of wood, and always fixed firmly at top and bottom.

I have said that, on the whole, the last fifty years have seen a great improvement in the treatment of bells and belfries; but only so lately as 1897, a recent writer, a keen ringer and expert in all relating to bells, had occasion to re-echo Mr. Lukis' complaints. He points out, however, that the Central Council of Ringers, then recently formed, is doing excellent work by its reports on bell-hanging and similar matters.

Some of these remarks of Mr. A. H. Cocks, in his great work on Buckinghamshire bells, are so admirable and so instructive that I cannot forbear to quote them. He devotes himself to finding out the reasons *why bells crack*; and his conclusion is that such a thing *rarely happens except from sheer neglect*. Further, that while the sexton and ringers may be entrusted with the actual care and use of the bells, the real responsibility lies, in the first place, with the incumbent of the parish, and, in a lesser degree, with the churchwardens. The incumbent, it should be remembered, has the legal right of granting or refusing access to the bells, and of saying when they shall or shall not be rung.

"If all incumbents," he says, "would remember that bell-hangings are *machines*, even if not quite so complicated as a steam-engine, and that all machines want a *little* attention, the lamentable and disgraceful state of many of the belfries would cease; and we bell-hunters would no longer get the almost stereotyped, semi-apologetic statement, on making our request for the key, 'I'm afraid you will find a great mess up there, but, to tell you the truth, I have never been up to them.'" As he aptly points out, ringers, who usually visit towers where the bells are ringable and everything in order, know little of these neglected places; but it is the incumbent's duty to know what goes on under his supposed charge; and if he refuses, the authority of rural deans and archdeacons should step in to arouse him to his duty.

Let every incumbent, then, who "has never been up," determine to visit his bells. He will doubtless find his trouble repaid, if they bear interesting inscriptions or devices; and if he finds the attempt attended by risk of life or limb, let him be persuaded to renew worn steps or broken ladder-rungs. If he finds the belfry or staircase full of animal and vegetable rubbish, let him take the simple but necessary step of fixing wire-netting over the windows, and cleanliness, once attained, should be easily preserved.

Plate 37.

Specimens of "Mixed Gothic" lettering
Used by Henry Jordan of London (1460). Reduced to about two-thirds size.

(See pages 13, 51.)

And now as to the cracking of bells, and how to prevent it. Bells may crack either at the top, or "crown," or at the rim, or "sound-bow," where the clapper strikes. The former is usually due to defective methods of hanging, which cannot be explained without becoming too technical; but the latter comes from a very simple and avoidable cause. Moreover, a bell cracked at the crown does not thereby lose its tone, and may last for years in that condition; but if cracked at the rim it is immediately and hopelessly ruined. If, again, the cannons, or metal loops by which the bell hangs from the wooden stock, should be broken, the bell may be kept sound by boring holes in the crown and bolting it to the stock. But in making this latter suggestion I do not wish to commend—rather to protest against—the practice of modern bell-founders, who do this in all cases, instead of using cannons. They are supported by the ringers, who say it makes the bell swing more easily; but it is a barbarous practice, and destroys the whole appearance of the bell.

Of all dangers which beset our unfortunate bells, by far the worst is the objectionable, but only too common, practice of "clocking," as it is called. Against this, no protests can be too strong. The reason is a very simple one. "Clocking" consists in tying the clapper to the rope in order to make the bell sound more easily and with little effort on the ringer's part. Now, this gives the clapper very little play, and it strikes continually on one place at very short intervals. This checks vibration and prevents the effect of the stroke from spreading, and is a sure cause of cracking at the rim sooner or later. Yet all over the country it is constantly being done, and on a recent visit to Essex it was my experience in tower after tower. Worse than that, I found the bells in several cases actually hung "dead," the stocks being fixed to the frames, so that any swinging was impossible.

"Clocking" is, unfortunately, no new practice, as we hear of it at Reading three hundred years ago; but would that modern churchwardens would take the same view of it that the good Joseph Carter, churchwarden of S. Lawrence and bell-founder, did then. He got the vicar to draft a resolution that, "Whereas there was, through the slothfulness of the sexton in times past, a kind of tolling the bell by the clapper-rope, it was now forbidden and taken away, and that the bell should be tolled as in times past and not in any such idle sort." In London alone twenty-eight large bells in the principal churches were cracked by "clocking" between 1820 and 1860.

Even the ordinary clock-hammer, striking on the upper side of the rim of the bell, often has the same effect; and for the same reason. But in both cases there is a remedy, if put in hand at once and after consulting a good bell-hanger, namely, that of "quarter-turning," or turning the bell round through one quarter of its circumference, so that the clapper may strike on a place at right angles to the old one, if that has become worn.

If, however, a bell has once become hopelessly cracked, there is no remedy but recasting into a new one; though it is said that a cracked bell in Dorset was successfully repaired by a Norwegian artificer about fifteen years ago, and where he has succeeded, others may yet. Nevertheless it is only too common for bells to be re-cast when there is no necessity. Perhaps one bell is broken, or it is desired to increase the number of the bells, and the founder, with a pardonable eye to business, suggests that all the old bells should be melted down, in order to have an entirely new ring, guaranteed in tune with each other. And thus disappears many an interesting and valuable old bell, perfectly sound and well-toned. It does not follow that because a bell is old its tone is inferior to a new one, or that it cannot be fitted into a new ring. Rather, the contrary is the case, and tone improves and mellows with age.

Plate 38.

Part of a Seventeenth Century Bell by Henry Oldfield of Nottingham.
The lettering is an imitation of mediaeval types, but the ornament is
characteristic of the later period.

(*See pages 49, 53.*)

But when all else fails, and re-casting is absolutely unavoidable, let me plead that some faithful record of the old bell may be kept. At least the old inscription may be preserved, as to their credit was often done by the seventeenth-century founders, on the new bell. This practice, I note, is increasing, and deserves every commendation. But there is an even more excellent way. The inscription may be copied in exact fac-simile on the new bell (with, of course, an indication of the new date), as has been successfully done in many instances, notably by Blews of Birmingham on the old tenor at Brailes, Warwickshire, and in other cases by Mears and Stainbank and by Taylor (see Plate 19). Or, again, the inscription-band may be cut out and kept in the church, or used as the ring of a candelabrum. This has been done at Chester-le-Street, in Durham; West Bergholt, in Essex; and elsewhere. It at least preserves what is of special interest and beauty. Or, lastly, the old bell may be kept in its entirety, as a relic of the past, in some part of the church. This has been done, to the great credit of the parish authorities at Wingrave, in Bucks; Batcombe, in Dorset; Barrow Gurney, in Somerset; and Swyncombe, in Oxfordshire. This may perhaps be a counsel of perfection, as it entails the sacrifice of the money allowed for the old metal; but it is certainly the most praiseworthy course, even if it is too much to expect from a poor parish.

I plead, therefore, in conclusion, first for clean and accessible belfries; secondly for orderly ringing-chambers; thirdly for due care and attention to the bells and their fittings; and last, but not least, for the preservation of all old and interesting bells, not only to earn the gratitude of the casual antiquary, but to show that their historic value, and the services they have so long and faithfully rendered, receive due appreciation.

INDEX

A

A. H. Cocks *69*
Ancient Uses Of Bells *37*
Angelus Bell *46*

B

Bagleys *17*
Bartlet *17*
Belfries *29, 34, 36, 56, 66, 69, 73*
Bell At Aldbourne *56*
Bell At Caversfield *5*
Belleyeteres *10, 49*
Bell-Founders *10, 11, 15, 54, 65*
Bell-Founding *8, 10, 15, 17*
Bell-Metal *6, 10*
Bells At Brailes *60*
Bells At Croyland *5*
Bells Of Exceptional Size *20*
Bells Of Rylstone *58*
Bergholt *73*
Blews *22, 73*
Brasyers *13, 53*
Bristol *10, 13, 15, 17, 49, 57*
Bury St. Edmunds *13, 15, 26*

C

Campana *1, 53, 54*
Campanalogy *1*
Campanile *20, 25, 29, 45, 47*
Campanile At Worcester *29*
Campaniles *20, 29*
Carillons *20, 26, 44*
Casting *1, 6, 10, 11, 12, 14, 17, 20, 26, 64, 73*
Change-Ringing *3, 31, 32, 34, 36, 52, 66*
Chimes *10, 20, 26, 44*

Chiming *31*
Christopher Hodson *22*
Cliburys *17*
Cors *53*
Cracking Of Bells *71*
Curfew Bell *46*
Customs Of Bells *37*

D

Decoration Of Bells *49*
Detached Towers *29*
Divine Service *37*
Dr. Raven *25, 26*

E

East Bergholt *29, 50*
Exeter Cathedral *33*

F

Fabian Stedman *32*
Fire Bell *37, 48*
Founders *6, 8, 10, 11, 13, 15, 17, 24, 25, 26, 49, 52, 53, 56, 58, 60, 63, 73*
Foundries *10, 12, 13, 15, 17, 49, 51*

G

Gleaning Bell *37, 46*
Gloucester Foundry *13, 17*
Goring *10, 56*
Great Bell Of Tong *22, 38, 48*

H

Henry Farmer *60*
Henry Jordan *13, 24, 49, 70*

I

Idbury *Vii, 39, 61*
Inscriptions *1, 5, 6, 13, 49, 51, 53, 56, 58, 60, 63, 64, 69*

J

Johannes De Copgrave *13*
John Bird *22*
John Bunyan *34*
John Danyell *13*

John Tonne *49, 67*
Joseph Carter *71*

L

Leicester *11, 13, 15, 19, 22, 51, 53, 60*
Lincolnshire *15, 25, 26, 43, 56*
London *5, 10, 13, 17, 20, 21, 22, 24, 25, 26, 27, 34, 49, 51, 53, 63, 64, 65, 70, 71*

M

Mears *17, 18, 22, 26*
Mears And Stainbank *Vii, 18, 25, 73*
Mearses *18*
Methods Of Ringing *39*
Michael Darbie *17*
Miles Graye *15, 17*
Modern Bell-Founder *8*
Modern Bell-Founders *1, 71*
Modern Uses Of Bells *37*

N

Newcombes *60*

O

Oldfields *15*

P

Pancake Bell *42*
Passing Bell *44*
Prayer Book *37, 46*

R

Rev. W. C. Lukis *36, 66*
Richard Phelps *25*
Richard Tunnoc *8, 13*
Rings Of Bells *2, 3, 17*
Robert Mot *17, 27, 53*
Rudhalls *63*

S

Sacring Bell *39, 57, 59*
Sanctus Bell *39, 61*
Science Of Bell-Ringing *1*
Secular Uses Of Bells *46*

Sermon Bell *39*
Signa *20*
Stainbank *18*
Stephen *15*
Stephen Norton *12*
Suffolk *10, 15, 29, 50*

T

Taylor *Vii, 19, 20, 22, 25, 33, 35, 38, 40, 73*
Tellers *44*
Tennyson *41, 62*
Thomas Hancox *53*
Tobie Norris *56, 58*
Tong *22, 31, 36*
Trade-Marks *13, 53*

U

Uses Of Bells *44*

W

William Culverden *13, 24*
William The Conqueror *44*
Worcester *5, 11, 12, 13, 15, 17, 25, 26, 29, 49, 53, 64*
Wymbishes *10*

Lector House believes that a society develops through a two-fold approach of continuous learning and adaptation, which is derived from the study of classic literary works spread across the historic timeline of literature records. Therefore, we aim at reviving, repairing and redeveloping all those inaccessible or damaged but historically as well as culturally important literature across subjects so that the future generations may have an opportunity to study and learn from past works to embark upon a journey of creating a better future.

This book is a result of an effort made by Lector House towards making a contribution to the preservation and repair of original ancient works which might hold historical significance to the approach of continuous learning across subjects.

HAPPY READING & LEARNING!

LECTOR HOUSE LLP
E-MAIL: lectorpublishing@gmail.com